Environmental Taxes

Environmental Taxes

An Introductory Analysis

Kalle Määttä

Professor of Law and Economics, University of Joensuu, Finland

Edward Elgar
Cheltenham, UK • Northampton, MA, USA

Published by
Edward Elgar Publishing Limited
Glensanda House
Montpellier Parade
Cheltenham
Glos GL50 1UA
UK

Edward Elgar Publishing, Inc.
136 West Street
Suite 202
Northampton
Massachusetts 01060
USA

A catalogue record for this book
is available from the British Library

ISBN-13: 978 1 84376 669 8
ISBN-10: 1 84376 669 8

Printed and bound in Great Britain by MPG Books Ltd, Bodmin, Cornwall

Contents

Preface

Studying environmental tax problems and theory of regulation has been largely a matter of coincidence for me, or fate, as many people would claim. My doctoral dissertation *Environmental Taxes: From an Economic Idea to a Legal Institution* (1997) was not the end but rather the beginning of a long and winding road. Thereafter, a great many of my books and articles have somehow been concerned with regulatory problems, some of them in relation to environmental taxes. This book contains some of the main points of those studies.

Discussions with many people have helped me to understand how to make a study which is critical from the law-making point of view. I am indebted particularly to Professors Kurt Deketelaere, Rainer Prokisch and Michael Rodi and Research Director Juha Honkatukia, for many helpful suggestions. I can only say that it is not their fault if the advice they provided was not always followed.

It has been a great pleasure to work with Roy Goldblatt, who assisted with the English translation. Our research assistant Lasse Pöyry has been of enormous help in many ways in preparing the research.

Edward Elgar Publishing Ltd has been efficient and flexible in its work. I therefore owe a special debt of gratitude to the Senior Commissioning Editor Dymphna Evans, Commissioning Editor Catherine Elgar and Editorial Assistant David Vince. I am also grateful to the Jenny and Antti Wihuri Foundation for the research grant they have provided for this study.

However, I reserve my greatest appreciation to my wife, Heidi, and of course, to Hanna, Matias and Ville.

Kalle Määttä
University of Joensuu, 2005

Abbreviations

BOD	biological oxygen demand
CFC	chlorofluorocarbon
DKK	Danish crown
Ds.	Departmentsskrivelse (ministry report, Sweden)
EU	European Union
HE	hallituksen esitys (government bill, Finland)
IEA	International Energy Agency
Km.	komitean mietintö (Committee Report, Finland)
NOU	Norges offentlige utredninger (Norwegian Official Commission)
OECD	Organization for Economic Co-operation and Development
R&D	research and development
SOU	Statens offentliga utredningar (Public Federal Studies, Sweden)
UK	United Kingdom
VAT	value-added tax

1. Introduction

1.1 THE PURPOSE OF THE STUDY

According to the Tinbergen rule, a different instrument has to be chosen for every goal. In spite of this rule, this study has two goals. First, the purpose is to analyse the way in which environmental taxes may be categorized and which factors affect the effectiveness and efficiency of different kinds of environmental tax in practice.

Environmental taxes deviate from each other according to the functions they serve and the manner in which they are implemented. From this point of view, analysing the appropriateness of environmental taxes should often be made case by case. As a result, the pragmatic approach is emphasized in the study.

The multiplicity of regulatory problems is also emphasized. At what level should the environmental tax rate be set? What is the proper time schedule for introducing an environmental tax? What are the most appropriate taxable characteristics and how should they be determined? What activities should be exempted from environmental taxation? How can tax relief be implemented? In which circumstances may environmental taxes be used as an adjunct to other environmental policy instruments? These are only some of the regulatory problems explored in this study.

Second, the approach that has been adopted is the theory of regulation. The normative theory of regulation is the benchmark here and concentrates on analysing the most appropriate design of legislation, which is tax legislation. For instance, different kinds of 'yardstick' are introduced to compare regulatory options. Moreover, the appropriateness of regulatory options is highlighted against the empirical evidence whenever possible.

In spite of the great importance of the normative theory, we should admit that legislators do not necessarily act to further public interest. In other words, the legislator may be influenced by interest groups. Therefore, the need for a positive theory of regulation is emphasized. An essential question involves the functions of positive theories of regulation with respect to issues related to drafting legislation.

It is astonishing how little time and effort lawyers and legal researchers devote to the questions related to the theory of regulation. In practice legal studies have concentrated on legal dogmatics. This study, however, claims that regulation theory would enrich legal studies as well as argumentation concerning the interpretation of laws. Theory of regulation teaches us to analyse legal problems in a future-oriented way, which is important in the dynamic world in which we live.

Briefly, the purpose of the study is to help lawyers see the wood for the trees; on the other hand, it aims to help economists and environmental politicians see the trees for the wood.

1.2 BASIC QUESTION

'To regulate or not to regulate, and if yes, then how?' These are the questions. The statement describes the basic questions the legislator has to answer when evaluating the need and appropriateness for regulation. The statement also reveals the concern of this study, namely issues related to drafting laws. More theoretically, it is a question about the theory of regulation.[1]

One purpose of the theory of regulation is to create opportunities to improve the quality of regulation. Another is to create opportunities for improving the stability of regulation.[2] Notwithstanding these goals, we should emphasize that the traditional approach in legal studies – legal dogmatics – is rather limited in analysing the issues concerning the preparation of laws. Legal dogmatics is an area of study which is essentially backward-looking in nature and thus cannot respond to the problems of social change.[3] Other tools are necessary for tackling the future-oriented questions relating to the 'evolutionary process' of a new legal institution. The framework which has been adopted in this study draws primarily on economics and environmental and tax policy.[4] Therefore, framing a question here can be characterized briefly in two interdependent ways. On the one hand, the theory of regulation – both normative and positive – has been used as a toolbox in the analysis of environmental taxes. On the other hand, environmental taxes have been used as an example of how to further develop the theory of regulation. Nevertheless, legal dogmatics cannot be avoided when a new institution is integrated into the existing legal system or the old institution is modified. An instance of this would be, for example, whether a new tax law is compatible with the prohibition on retroactive tax legislation according to constitutional law. Moreover, several intractable problems may arise due to the EU law concerning the prohibition of discriminatory taxation. The existing legal system may be seen as a constraint in such cases where a new legal institution is grafted onto the existing one.[5]

What are the options in this case? First, a new legal institution can be integrated into the existing legal system without preserving its special character. Thus, the new institution is actually treated in terms of the old. This is referred to as the 'continuity principle'. Another option would be for a new legal institution to maintain its special character (to some extent) when it is integrated into an existing legal system. This may simply be labelled the 'non-continuity principle'.

As we are concentrating on the theory of regulation, we will omit the points of view related to the problems of legal interpretation. Consequently, interesting questions concerning regulation of state aid and prohibition of discriminatory taxation are not covered in this study.[6] Moreover, all constitutional issues related to environmental taxes have been ignored. According to Wienert (1997), the following questions are important to regulatory reform: Should we regulate? For instance, this may involve deregulation, which denotes the complete or partial elimination of regulation in a sector. Or it may be concern reregulation, which denotes a case in which existing regulation is replaced by new or is redesigned. In practice, the key challenge is often not choosing between regulation and no regulation, but redesigning unnecessarily disruptive regulation.[7]

How should we regulate? Above all, this includes issues related to designing specific regulatory measures, such as environmental taxes. The statement that 'the devil is in details' clearly indicates how important this point of view is. An important dimension is the interaction between different forms of regulation.

When should we regulate? The timing of regulation is often ignored in research, even though in practice it may be an important factor. For instance, delays in regulation are critical. Delay in regulation can be divided into four sub-delays:

- a delay in observation is the period between an event demanding regulation or its amendment and the point in time when the event is noted;
- a delay in decision-making is the period between the observation of the event and the time when the decision to introduce or amend regulation is made;
- a delay in implementation is the time lag before the new or reformed regulation is put into effect after resolution;
- a delay in effect is the period between the implementation of regulation and the point in time when its effects occur.

At which level – local, national or supranational – should we regulate? Since markets have become more international, it is becoming increasingly difficult for domestic authorities to control the behaviour of their national private sector actors. It is also increasingly difficult for national governments to achieve the intended goals of regulation. On the other hand, supranational regulation is not without practical problems.

1.3 FROM A PROBLEM TO A GOAL

Regulation of course is not a goal in itself. Its aim is to influence some state of affairs; in other words, to solve certain problems in society. For instance, as far as environmental protection is concerned, the economic rationale of regulation often rests on negative externalities caused by pollution or the use of resources. More formally, an externality exists whenever the welfare of some agent, either a firm or household, depends directly or indirectly on his or her activities and on the activities controlled by some other agent as well.[8] Under these circumstances, the benefits or the costs of the exchange may spill over onto other parties than those explicitly engaged in the exchange. From this point of view, we may speak about external benefits (positive externalities) and external costs (negative externalities). The presence of negative externalities leads to market failure, for example, a firm which produces too much and at prices too low for the efficient allocation of resources in the economy. More generally, if legal norms correct market imperfections and thus improve the efficiency of resource allocation, they can be labelled 'efficiency norms'. Another main group of legal norms consists of equity norms, which aim at correcting inequitable market practices. For instance, progressive income taxation schedules and lower value-added tax (VAT) rates on necessities represent equity norms.[9]

The Pigouvian approach can be understood to mean that some form of state intervention is necessary to correct market failures.[10] Coase challenged this view in his 1960 article 'The Problem of Social Cost'. Coase emphasized that in the presence of well-defined property rights and if transaction costs are small enough, the affected parties can negotiate with each other and agree on an efficient allocation of resources. In other words, no intervention from the public side is needed to control market failures except the creation of well-defined property rights and arrangements which guarantee that transaction costs would not be an obstacle to negotiations.

The solution proposed by Coase may be significant in the context of small-group externalities, where there are only a few affected parties and their respective rights have been clearly defined. In contrast, in the case of mass externalities Coase's recommendation is practically impossible, and there is usually a clear need for public intervention.[11] However, Coase's thoughts cannot be ignored completely, even in the context of mass externalities. It can be claimed that the Pigouvian approach is characterized by regulation optimism, which holds implicitly that markets are imperfect, but government is perfect. The attitude to regulation, however, became more pragmatic following the publication of Coase's article: governments can fail as well as markets.[12] The approach adopted here is best also characterized as pragmatic.

There has also been controversy over the need for policy goals when enacting new laws. For instance, Hourcade and Baron (1993) have claimed that the absence of goals is not necessarily a weakness in legislation. According to them, the advantage of such a system is that legislation can be introduced without prior agreement on either the end result or the respective contributions of those liable under legislation. Although enacting legislation without any clear regulatory goal poses no obstacles, arguments do exist which fall short of advocating Hourcade and Baron's claim. For instance, precisely defined goals in legal regulation can at the very least promote rational discussion about the possibilities of reaching these goals.[13] The policy option recommended by Hourcade and Baron also flies in the face of the general principle in taxation stating that taxpayers should as much as possible be able to clearly see what it is being taxed and also understand the purpose the tax is intended to serve.[14]

Policy goals may vary extensively case by case. It is possible to aim, for example, at prohibiting some activity totally. The goal, however, is usually to only reduce undesirable behaviour, not to eliminate it totally. The fiscal side of the coin in this case is that if environmental taxes are applied, they will usually generate revenue. Finally, even though a problem exists, it is possible that no intervention is made (and no policy goals are set), if the problem is small and the costs connected with intervention are large. While a clear specification of the objectives to be achieved by regulation may be important for managing the appropriate environmental tax policy, it is, however, a manifold problem.

First, the objectives of regulation are not necessarily determined in a clear-cut way. For instance, drafts of the Finnish energy tax laws have at a very general level noted the improved state of the environment as one of the purposes of the law.[15] Second, in certain situations there have been too many objectives related to the number of instruments applied, which is contrary to the Tinbergen rule: for every goal a different instrument has to be chosen.[16] Third, in the discussion of the legislative goals, a distinction has to be made between explicit and actual goals. The explicit goals are openly expressed in the preparatory drafts of the legislation. However, the explicit goals do not necessarily correspond to the actual goals. Thus, one concept, legal illusion, may be cited to describe the situation in which the explicit and actual goals of laws deviate from each other. Furthermore, within the context of tax legislation we may speak about fiscal illusion.[17]

The notion of fiscal illusion is associated with the misperception of the fiscal burden, or the amount of tax paid. It usually refers to a positive version of fiscal illusion and means that taxpayers regard their tax burden as smaller than it actually is. There is also a negative version of fiscal illusion, where taxpayers perceive their tax burden in fact to be heavier. There are many potential sources of positive fiscal illusion: taxes can become incorporated into the price of the product, making the taxpayer largely unaware of the quantitative importance of the tax; the incidence of the tax may be unknown; the total tax revenue may be fragmented over a number of different taxes; persuasive definitions have also been mentioned in this context.[18] The principal source of fiscal illusion is the public's deficient information about the actual goals and effects of the legislation. On the other hand, we may also speak about ecological illusion. Ecological illusion refers to a situation in which the explicit legislative goal is to improve the state of the environment but in fact it is only a symbolic gesture, a 'salving of conscience', or the actual purpose is to improve the competitive position of domestic industry instead of the environment. As an example, Poterba (1993) has noted that part of the appeal of the carbon tax is clearly political: enacting a tax enables politicians to claim that they have taken immediate action on the global warming problem.[19]

1.4 FROM A GOAL TO AN INSTRUMENT CHOICE AND INSTRUMENT DESIGN

The first task in choosing an instrument is to outline the alternative types of regulation on a comparative basis. Instruments which reasonably compete with each other are referred to as 'a choice set'.[20] In practice, instruments may be both substitutes and complements for one another. When instruments are substitutes, environmental policy goals could be promoted in a variety of way (separately), such as direct regulation, environmental taxes, emissions trading, environmental subsidies or voluntary means.[21] When instruments are complementary, one instrument may reinforce the effectiveness of another or one type may be used to speed up the measures required by the forthcoming regulation.

For the purpose of this study only a rough description of the most central instruments is necessary. Policy instruments have traditionally been divided into two main groups: regulatory and economic instruments. Regulatory instruments in environmental policy are described by Opschoor and Vos (1989) as 'institutional measures aimed at directly influencing the environmental performance of polluters by regulating processes or products used, by limiting the discharge of certain pollutants, and/or by restricting activities to certain times, areas, etc., through licensing, setting of standards, zoning, etc'. Regulatory instruments are also called 'direct regulation'.

Economic (that is market-based or market-oriented) instruments have been characterized in various ways. It has been pointed out that the incentive concept is characteristic of economic instruments, or that these instruments affect the costs and benefits of alternative actions on economic agents, thereby influencing the decision-making; in addition attention has been paid to financial transfers between economic agents and the community or to the actual creation of new markets.[22] Environmental taxes, emissions trading and environmental subsidies have usually been classified as economic instruments.

The decision-making process concerning instrument choice and design can be divided into two levels: the macro-policy and micro-policy level. At the macro-policy level, it is assumed that the legislator has an outline for viable instruments though there is no exact specification of their design. At the micro-policy level, the decisions are formulated to permit a legislative revision of the instrument selected at the macro-policy level. For instance, decisions such as the tax rate level to be set, the schedule for introducing new legislation, the scope of the legislation and the activities to be exempted from the legislation are all regulatory problems confronted at the micro-policy level. Economists have often remained at the macro-policy level in their analysis of policy instruments. In other words, they have paid little attention to the administrative and legal issues concerning the implementation of legislation.

Bracewell-Milnes (1992) has claimed that there is a risk in the micro-policy approach. Consideration of major questions may be ignored due to concentration on technical discussions concerning the form of legislation most suited to the purpose. Consequently, the best regulatory options may be passed over. Although Bracewell-Milnes's opinion should be borne in mind with regard to legal decision-making, he exaggerates the risks and understates the importance of decisions at the micro-policy level. Studying the design issues connected with legislation provides a more objective picture of the relevant legal norms compared with other instruments. Taking these questions into account is a way of minimizing the risk of regulatory failures.[23] If the ideal legislation and its theoretical virtues are compared with the alternative instruments with their practical defects, it is likely that the aforementioned instrument would be preferred to other instruments, and, at least in some cases, incorrectly.[24] Consideration of the micro-policy issues should thus be seen as a way of making the comparison between different instruments more transparent and trustworthy. This is due to the feedback between the micro-policy and macro-policy levels. The answer to the 'major questions' cited by

Bracewell-Milnes at the macro-policy level depends crucially on the decisions concerning the design of an instrument. Taking micro-policy issues seriously also makes it possible to reduce the regulatory gap between researchers and legislators. As Schelling (1983) notes, researchers – referring only to economists – have been aware of all the theoretical virtues of certain kinds of legislation, whereas legislators and administrators have been aware of all the practical difficulties involved in their implementation. This regulatory gap may have been one key reason why the economists' voice was not heard and environmental taxes were adopted slowly, especially in the 1970s and 1980s. On the other hand, an examination of micro-policy issues will suggest fruitful avenues for extending the boundaries of existing theory beyond environmental taxes.[25]

Regulatory standards are needed, both at the macro-policy and micro-policy levels, when competing regulations are compared.[26] In recent years, a wide scale of regulatory standards in policy-making has been established, for example, in the preparatory drafting of legislation,[27] in OECD studies and surveys,[28] as well as by certain researchers. Four categories of regulatory standards have been formulated: regulatory effectiveness, flexibility, efficiency and equity.[29] They may also be called standards or features of good legislation.

An essential standard with respect to every instrument in every policy field is regulatory effectiveness, or the ability to achieve the desired goals within a given time schedule. In the case of environmental policy instruments, such as environmental taxes, this standard is called 'environmental effectiveness'. In addition to the goals of legislation and achieving them, the side-effects, be they detrimental or beneficial, should also be taken into account. The question of side-effects arises, for instance, when the restriction of nitrogen oxide's by a nitrogen oxide's tax leads to an increase in nitrous oxide emissions (detrimental effects), or when a sulphur tax leads to a reduction of sulphur dioxide and carbon dioxide emissions (beneficial effects). Moreover, competitive disadvantages due to an environmental tax may be regarded as detrimental side-effects, whereas the possibility of reducing distortive taxes through revenues from environmental taxes, or a double-dividend gain, may be regarded as a beneficial side-effect.

From the environmental effectiveness point of view, a distinction between explicit and implicit instruments is worth making. By explicit instruments we mean those instruments whose goal is explicitly to influence the state of affairs. For instance, a carbon tax on fossil fuels is intended to reduce carbon dioxide emissions. Implicit instruments are not intended primarily to affect the state of affairs in question, for example, to reduce carbon dioxide emissions, but they actually affect this state of affairs in both predictable and unpredictable ways. An instance of this is the petrol tax, which has been levied in many countries longer than the problems caused by carbon dioxide emissions have been known. The distinction between incentive and fiscal environmental taxes is based on a more general distinction between explicit and implicit instruments.

The concept of flexibility may be divided into three aspects.[30] First, external flexibility can be defined as the ability of a policy instrument to react to changes in external circumstances.[31] Technological progress, inflation, price fluctuations of certain products, increases in the number of economic agents and amendments to the legislation are examples of changes in external circumstances. External flexibility is an important regulatory standard because it takes time – often due to political reasons – to amend regulation, which threatens the implementation of policy goals. Moreover, uncertainty over the legislation and its amendment caused by external inflexibility is a problem. Economic growth is one factor which has to be considered in this respect. Expanding production of old and new firms will require a rise in environmental taxes if environmental policy goals are to be maintained. From this point of view, environmental taxes are externally inflexible, which may also erode their environmental effectiveness. On the contrary, under emissions trading, market forces automatically accommodate themselves to economic growth with no increase in pollution.

Second, a policy instrument is normatively more flexible, the more easily it can be amended or corrected at any given point of time.[32] On the other hand, one problem of normatively flexible regulation is that such legislation may not be stable. Third, the more a policy instrument covers the technical measures needed to reduce pollution, the more flexible it is technologically. Technical measures may constitute installing pollution abatement technology, improving production efficiency and changing processes to reduce the use of polluting substances.[33]

Efficiency properties of regulation may be analysed from at least three points of view. Cost-effectiveness implies that the policy goal is achieved at as low a cost as possible.[34] The relationship between regulatory effectiveness and cost-effectiveness should also be recognized and acknowledged: the more ambitious the environmental policy is, the higher the costs from reducing pollution are; thus, the need for cost-effective instruments in environmental policy increases in these circumstances. The concern over rising marginal abatement costs is clearly visible in the development of environmental tax policy. This can be read directly in the preparatory legislative drafts, for instance, in Denmark, Finland, Norway and Sweden. Therefore, cost-effectiveness has become an essential factor legitimating environmental taxes. In spite of this, the empirical evidence for this property is not very common with respect to environmental taxes. Most of the studies that have been made concern the cost-ineffectiveness of direct regulation as compared with the least-cost allocation of abatement. Nevertheless, we cannot conclude on this basis that environmental taxes, in effect, would even approach the least-cost means of reducing pollution.

Dynamic efficiency refers here to how well policy instruments encourage the search for and adoption of new technology. An instrument is dynamically more efficient when there are greater incentives to develop and implement innovations.[35] The problem here is that virtually all regulation, among them environmental taxes, which affects output, profitability and technological constraints also have implications for innovative activities, positive or negative. However, the purpose here is not to 'test' empirically whether environmental taxes are efficient from the dynamic point of view. Instead, we can state that at least the following factors may be important in evaluating the dynamic efficiency of regulation. First, the more flexible regulation is technologically, the better the opportunities it provides for creative activities as well as the diffusion of innovations. Second, regulation may adversely affect innovation by forcing firms to make additional expenditures or outlays. Third, the larger the expected net return from innovation is, the better the opportunities to promote innovative activities are. Finally, uncertainty adversely affects innovation. From the regulatory point of view, uncertainties may concern the conduct to be regulated, the timing and stringency of controls, and the costs of compliance.[36]

Administrative efficiency implies the minimization of administrative costs incurred by both regulators and regulatees. Certain administrative solutions may be critical with respect to the level of these costs. For instance, quite a large portion of environmental taxes in force today can be seen as adoptions of existing fiscal structures to environmental purposes.[37] Moreover, many environmental taxes have been 'piggy-backed' onto direct regulation.[38]

In spite of its ambiguity, one important regulatory standard is equity. It impacts on income distribution: it is the economic burden created by the regulation regressive, proportional or progressive in its distributional consequences?[39] Moreover, neutrality requires that a policy instrument does not influence the competitive conditions between firms in any way other than the desired policy grounds.[40] More specifically, domestic and foreign enterprises, old and new facilities, small and large firms, as well as private and public enterprises, should be treated equally according to this regulatory standard. Violations of neutrality are often reduced to a phenomenon known as 'regulatory capture', that is the authorities act in the interest of the regulated rather than the public interest.[41] There may also be concerns about regional distribution of environmental taxes, some regions of the country bearing a larger burden than others.[42]

Despite the importance of regulatory standards, we must admit that they have their restrictions.[43] First, not all the criteria can be used in a quantitative sense: it is not always possible to quantify a degree of accomplishment. For instance, such a criterion reflects different dimensions of flexibility. Second, we cannot expect that a single regulatory option is superior to all others in respect to every criterion. In other words, different criteria do not usually coincide. It is therefore necessary to assign relative weights to the importance of individual criteria, which is, however, difficult. Finally, the determination of the standards of a good legal system in an exhaustive way is impossible.[44] Nevertheless, regulatory standards create a basis for resolving regulatory problems or at least showing that it is impossible to resolve these problems unambiguously. In any case, they can be applied to narrow the scope of appropriate regulations. In this way policy-making is usually described as a two-stage process. The first stage is to set goals which define the level at which society is to be protected. The second stage is to then select the instrument which is most suitable for achieving these goals. However, separating goals and instruments in this way gives a simplistic picture of the interaction between the two stages. For instance, Nichols (1984) has claimed that the appropriate target often depends on the policy instrument to be used. Segerson (1996) has emphasized the contrasting view that the choice of goals and instruments should be made simultaneously, since instrument choice can affect the overall cost of achieving a given goal and thus affect the goal itself.

1.5 OUTLINING THE POSITIVE THEORY OF REGULATION

If the regulation is applied solely in response to the demand of the public for the correction of inefficient or inequitable market practices, the normative theory of regulation would be sufficient in a study serving issues concerning drafting legislation. In other words, recommendations will be made as to how the legislator should act to further public interest. In the current context, this would mean that the study is limited to the specification of regulatory standards and the normative analysis of legislation. However, the legislator may also be influenced by interest groups and it may be the interests of these groups, not the public interest, which is promoted by the legislation.[45] What is needed is a positive theory of regulation.

Positive studies of instrument choice try to explain why one instrument or a combination of instruments has been chosen in a particular context. One famous theorem concerning the choice between environmental taxes and regulatory instruments is the Buchanan–Tullock theorem.[46] This theorem states that the explanation for the predominance of the regulatory approach in environmental policy lies in the different costs for firms under the alternative instruments. Direct regulation imposes lower costs on firms than an equivalent environmental tax, which causes polluters to favour direct regulation over taxes. On the other hand, the profits of existing firms are increased, because under direct regulation new sources of pollution are regulated more stringently than existing sources. Consequently, one message is clear: interest groups have a significant influence on legislation. In spite of the desire to explain the actual choice of instrument, relatively little attention has been paid to one essential question: what are the functions of a positive theory of regulation with respect to drafting legislation? A positive theory may serve the following three functions.[47]

The first function of the positive theories is to outline the legitimacy strategies for new or modified legislation. By analysing the factors behind the emergence of legal policy it is possible to determine which types of arrangements – called legitimacy strategies – make new forms of legislation acceptable to the target groups of legislation as well as to the public. The interaction between the normative and the positive side of the study is expressed here. To what extent is it possible to apply legitimacy strategies without the theoretical virtues of legislation suffering from their application? In any case, the normative approach is required when the appropriateness of different legitimacy strategies is analysed. In addition, the normative theory of regulation may offer a tool for best preventing inappropriate aims influencing the content of legislation.

The second function of positive theories is to search for a means to minimize adjustment costs, that is the costs of moving from a situation without a new institution in the legal system to one in which a new institution has been incorporated. The significance of this has been clearly expressed by the Meade Committee (Meade, 1978), which emphasized the fact that attention should not be paid to the quality of the tax system alone but also to the ease or difficulties of the transitional problems.

The third function of positive theories is to improve the stability of legislation. In other words, the analysis of factors behind the adoption or non-adoption of new legislation offers opportunities to find pitfalls which threaten stable policy. The importance of stable legislation has to be emphasized, in particular, due to the regulatory character of the legislation; for example, to provide long-term investors a degree of security that future policy changes will not undermine their efforts. Regulatory effectiveness as well as the efficiency properties of legislation would suffer significantly from an unstable policy. Thus, stable and predictable legislation is crucial to the practical achievement of the theoretical advantages of legislation.[48]

Therefore, with regard to the legislative issues, policy certainty achieves a similar position to legal certainty in the application of the law. It is not sufficient to prevent arbitrariness in the application of the law and for court decisions to be correct. If laws are enacted in unexpected ways at short notice, the target groups will have no opportunity to react to the changes in the legal environment, and the theoretical virtues of the legislation will be eroded.

NOTES

1   See Ogus (1994) and Ogus (2001), and Määttä (1997) on the theory of regulation.
2   See Meade (1978), 3.
3   See Aarnio (1978), 58.
4   See Anderson et al. (1977), 2, and Faure, Vervaele and Weale (1994), 6–7.
5   See Määttä (1997), 3–4.
6   See van Calster (2003), 311 ff.
7   See Määttä (2001), 9.
8   See Meade (1973), 15 ff.
9   Määttä (1997), 7.
10 See Pigou (1932), 131 ff.
11 See Regan (1972), 437, and Baumol and Oates (1988), 10.
12 See Coase (1988), 174 ff, and Stiglitz (1988), 7–8. On the pragmatic approach, see Posner (1995), 4 ff.
13 Klami (1977), 6–7.
14 Meade (1978), 19.
15 See Määttä (2003), 175 ff,
16 See Tinbergen (1952), 37 ff.
17 On fiscal illusion in general, see Puviani (1897) and (1903), and Buchanan (1967), 126 ff. On fiscal illusion under environmental taxation, Määttä (2004), 69 ff.
18 See Buchanan (1967), 132, Goetz (1977), 177–178, Messere (1993), 112, Barthold (1994), 138, and Heyndels and Smolders (1995), 127 ff.
19 See Deketelaere (1995), 169 ff.
20 See Bohm and Russell (1985), 455, Ogus (1994), 247–248, and OECD (1996), 11.
21 See Richards (2003), 61 ff.
22 See OECD (1980), 8, Opschoor and Vos (1989), 13, and OECD (1991), 10–11.
23 See Ogus (1994), 55–56.
24 See Oosterhuis and de Savornin Lohman (1994), 37.
25 Hahn (1989), 23. See also Milne (2003), 3 ff.
26 See Barde and Smith (1997), 24, and OECD (1997), 89 ff.
27 See SOU 1990:59, and NOU 1992:3, 16 ff.
28 See OECD (1991), 18 ff, and OECD (1994), 113–114.
29 See Hahn and Stavins (1992), 466.
30 See Määttä (1997), 16-17. and Meade (1978), 21, where a distinction has been made between economic and political flexibility. This distinction is not discussed here.
31 See Baumol and Oates (1988), 192.
32 See Rehbinder (1993), 60–61.
33 See OECD (1996), 11.
34 See Baumol and Oates (1971), 42 ff, and Tietenberg (1990), 17 ff.
35 See. Wenders (1975), 383 ff.
36 See Stewart (1981), 1256 ff.
37 See Smith (1992), 33, and Määttä (1997), 167.
38 See TemaNord 1996:568, 31–32.
39 See Meade (1978), 12 ff.
40 Deketelaere (1993), 48.
41 See Bohm and Russell (1985), 439.

42   See Stavins and Whitehead (1992), 20–21.
43   See OECD (1994), 114.
44   See also OECD (1997), 93.
45   Hahn (1989), 18.
46   See Buchanan and Tullock (1975), 139 ff.
47   Määttä (1997), 33–35.
48   See OECD (1996), 7.

2. Conceptual Framework

2.1 PRELIMINARY REMARKS

There is a Finnish saying that 'a good child has many names', and this is also the case with environmental taxes. They have been called pollution taxes, green taxes, ecological taxes, ecotaxes, Pigouvian taxes and environmental charges. Choosing the most appropriate one is ultimately a matter of taste and will not be discussed here. However, one issue is worth mentioning. When the payments polluters make are legally taxes, it is consistent to call them 'environmental taxes', not 'environmental charges'.

There may be difficulties in implementing the concept of an environmental tax, that is defining the scope of such taxes is inevitably imprecise. One reason behind the conceptual disorder may be that in different countries the concept has been introduced in the tax and environmental policy discussion without any academic discussion among legal researchers. On the other hand, these difficulties may not be so overwhelming that they threaten the existence of the whole concept. The best proof of this is the continuing use of the concept, even though its scope is far from established and clear-cut.

The OECD has done substantial by work commissioning surveys, studies and reports in the field of environmental taxation, and as a result some parameters for a concept of environmental taxes have been established. However, no unambiguous definition of the concept has arisen in these surveys. Some surveys have only covered taxes perceived as explicitly having an environmental purpose. Other studies deal with a number of areas in the tax system where the structure of existing taxes may have significant effects on the environment. There have also been attempts to make general definitions. For instance, according to OECD (1980), an environmental tax can be defined as 'a tax based on polluting emissions (for example BOD discharges) or on disamenities expressed by some appropriate method of measurement (for example an index of annoyance) or on other parameters such as inputs'. Commonly, environmental taxes are defined in legislation. This has been the case in the Ecotax Law in Belgium, where environmental tax is defined as 'taxe assimilée aux accizes, frappant un produit mis à la consomation en raison des nuisances écologiques qu'il est réputé générer'.[1]

On the other hand, in analysing the requirements for using the concept of environmental tax, it seems most appropriate to connect it to its legislative use. In other words, only such taxes should be labelled environmental taxes which are specifically called 'environmental taxes' in the law, as in the title of the tax law. However, this approach does not offer a totally coherent way of defining the scope of environmental taxes because the use of this concept varies between countries.

The specific environmental objective of the tax has often been crucial in defining the scope of environmental taxes. However, this purpose-related definition of environmental taxes has its own problems. The goals involved in the preparation of laws regulating environmental taxes may be obscure. It is not unusual that the goals of the laws are defined in quite general terms. On the other hand, it is possible that environmental reasons are only a way of making the tax more palatable, if the primary goal of the tax is fiscal. In other words, the legislator takes advantage of the fiscal illusion. Buchanan (1967) has expressed this point of view by stating that 'if a particular attitude is pervasive in the community, an opportunity is provided to levy a tax that will capitalise on such sentiment, making the burden appear less than might otherwise be the case'. Moreover, one source of definition problems is that taxes exist which have been introduced for non-environmental reasons but where environmental considerations have recently had to be taken into account in the structure of the tax. In addition, in some cases environmental considerations have only been included when amending part of the tax law. Both of these features have been familiar in energy taxation.[2]

How broad an interpretation should be given to the concept 'environment'? For instance, Bohm (1994) has stated that if environment is defined in a very broad sense, part of the excise taxes on alcohol (concerning its effect on the social environment), and taxes on tobacco (reducing the air quality of non-smokers), should be defined as environmental taxes. Messere (1993) has, perhaps tongue-in-cheek, also included taxes paid by dog-owners as environmental taxes. Many environmental taxes are related to pollution, that is they aim at reducing sulphur dioxide and carbon dioxide emissions, waste and other pollution in the environment. Moreover, environmental taxes may be associated with resource utilization, including the use of land or water resources. From this point of view, the term 'environmental tax' is an umbrella concept for two kinds of tax, pollution tax and resource tax.[3]

One borderline issue concerning the concept of tax arises from the tax expenditures or tax subsidies designed to provide incentives to reduce pollution. For instance, accelerated depreciation provisions in corporate income taxation, which provide incentives for the installation of certain types of pollution equipment, are such tax expenditures. More generally, tax expenditures are seen as departures from the normative tax structure (including VAT, income tax, and so on) and are designed to favour a particular business, activity, or class of persons. Here, environmentally motivated tax expenditures in income taxation are not included in the group of environmental taxes.[4] This is simply because they have the character of environmental subsidies rather than environmental taxes. This is emphasized by the fact that tax expenditures are the functional equivalent of direct expenditures, such as grants or soft loans for pollution equipment. Similarly, the lower VAT rate, for example, on electric cars has been classified as an environmental subsidy.

2.2 ENVIRONMENTAL TAXES AND CHARGES

There are considerable differences between taxes and charges (or fees) both in the legal sense and in respect of their use as environmental policy instruments.[5] Therefore, the aim here is to highlight the most essential differences between these financial measures. The borderlines between taxes and charges may vary from one country to another.[6] Nevertheless, we do not concentrate on these issues but analyse the issue on a more general level.

Taxes are unrequited payments in which benefits provided by governments to taxpayers are not normally in proportion to their payment. Charges are paid by individuals and companies to authorities in return for services received.[7] For instance, municipal waste user charges raising revenue for waste collection and disposal are payments for a service whereas waste taxes are not. The revenue generated by taxes goes to the general budget or is earmarked for a broad range of environmental expenditures. The difference can also be expressed to show, for instance, that waste water user charges are payments for the use of the sewage system, whereas water effluent taxes are levied regardless of where the waste water is discharged.[8]

Environmental charges can roughly be divided into user and administrative charges. User charges have been defined as payments to meet the costs of the collective or public treatment of effluent and waste, whereas administrative charges are payments for services to authority, for instance, for the registration of chemicals and enforcement of regulations. Administrative charges have been divided into licence fees and registration or control fees.[9]

The relationship between environmental taxes and environmental charges can be highlighted especially with respect to environmental policy matters. By definition, levying charges requires the existence of a public service providing benefits for users or customers; if no service exists, it is usually impossible to levy any charges. Hence, waste water charges have been criticized since they can be levied only on those polluters who release their waste waters to the sewage system, but not on those polluters who discharge them directly into open waters. From the environmental policy perspective, environmental taxes, for example, taxes on waste water, are superior to charges because they can be levied regardless of where the waste water is discharged.

The legal restrictions in setting the charge rate and the tax rate constitute an additional distinguishing factor. With respect to charges, the principle of prime cost is applied: charges can cover total expenditures from producing services but nothing more. With respect to taxes, in principle, there are no legal limits in setting the tax rate.[10] Therefore, owing to the principle of prime cost, the levels of charges may be so low that they provide little incentive for polluters to change their behaviour. It has been noted that the incentives of administrative charges have been small or absent in practice.[11] Fundamentally, the problem is whether to use the concept 'environmental tax' or 'environmental charge' for measures which are legally taxes. In the legislation of many countries and more generally in the literature, there is a singular lack of clarity with respect to this issue. Sometimes measures are called environmental taxes, sometimes environmental charges, and there is no clear rationale behind the choice.

The concept 'environmental charge' has been preferred for several reasons. First, the feeling is that the use of charge is important where a cost is involved; in this case in the form of damage to the environment which an actor, for instance, a firm or a household, causes. Second, it would be more consistent to use the term 'charge' to separate environmental charges from other selective taxes. Third, it has been claimed that one way to overcome resistance to the idea may be to indulge in semantics.[12] Finally, it has been noted that in regard to a rather large group of fiscal measures the concept 'charge' is used, although they are in legal terms 'taxes'.[13]

However, there are also strong arguments favouring the use of the concept 'tax' in this case. First, using the term 'environmental charge' may lead to confusion with respect to the legal character of environmental taxes. Second, and also partially related to the first argument, the objectives and the framework of an environmentally related tax must be clear. The use of the concept 'tax' would be more compatible with the transparency principle. Third, it is to some extent paradoxical to require the application of 'charge' on the basis that it would emphasize the regulatory nature of environmental taxes. For instance, user charges have a revenue-raising purpose, and administrative charges are usually also levied for revenue-raising purposes. Consequently, 'charge' may manifest the revenue-raising purpose rather than the regulatory purpose in the field of environmental policy. Finally, we might ask whether it is inconsistent to call environmental taxes 'taxes', if the legislative practice in a country is to call all taxes on products 'charges'.

However, there is another side to the issue. Is it justifiable to call product taxes charges at all, although this has been the tradition in tax legislation?

In summary, the concept 'tax' may be recommended in order to avoid any confusion with user and administrative charges. Moreover, the concept 'environmental charge' is not so well established to necessitate foregoing the concept 'environmental tax'.

2.3 INCENTIVE, FINANCING AND FISCAL ENVIRONMENTAL TAXES

One possibility here would be to discuss environmental taxes without distinguishing them according to their objectives. However, within this context a difference is made according to the motives expressed in the preparatory drafts of legislation concerning environmental taxes. In this way it is possible, simply, to analyse whether different kinds of environmental taxes have accomplished the objectives mentioned, for example in government bills. Of course, there may be difficulties in implementing this approach, among other things, since the objectives of environmental tax laws may not be determined in a clear-cut way.

Incentive environmental taxes are created in order to guide the behaviour of polluters, whereas their revenues are of secondary importance, if they have importance at all.[14] The tax level is determined by the desired goal of pollution reduction or a reduction in the use of natural resources. For instance, the sole purpose of tax differentiation, for example, tax differentiation between leaded and unleaded petrol, is its incentive impact. In addition, taxes on some disposable items, such as carrier bags, beverage containers, and disposable cameras and razors are examples of this group of environmental taxes. Incentive waste taxes are applied in several countries in order to minimize waste generation, discourage production and consumption of waste-intensive products, or/and promote recycling, which saves both depletable resources and space for waste dumping. Water effluent taxes are sometimes, but not necessarily always, the incentive for their primary intent.

Redistributive environmental taxes can also be classified as incentive taxes. It is characteristic of these taxes that tax proceeds are refunded to those liable to tax, for example, in the form of subsidies to environmental protection investments. Therefore, they are also called 'tax-cum-subsidy' schemes. The number of redistributive taxes is in practice low. On the other hand, redistributive environmental taxes have awakened interest in the environmental tax literature.[15]

Financing environmental taxes are revenue sources for financing environmental protection measures.[16] The tax level is determined by the revenue need for the measures. For instance, the costs of waste oil management for the collection, storage and disposal of used oil are covered by the waste oil tax on lubricants in some countries. Second, financing waste taxes are aimed at the proper collection, processing and storage of waste or restoration of old hazardous waste sites. Third, the amount of the water effluent tax may be based on the revenue requirements of specific public water treatment installations.[17] Unlike incentive environmental taxes, financing environmental taxes are not regulatory taxes, or taxes which are intended to change the behaviour of households and firms. Since the primary purpose of financing environmental taxes is to generate funds, they can be classified as fiscal taxes, similar in kind to income tax and value-added tax. Moreover, in some cases it is impossible to speak about incentive taxes or financing taxes. Rather, these taxes can be called mixed-type environmental taxes. For instance, a tax on NiCd batteries may be introduced, on the one hand, to generate revenue for financing the collection of used NiCd batteries, and, on the other hand, to make environmentally friendly batteries more competitive compared with NiCd batteries.

Fiscal environmental taxes are taxes which are primarily aimed at generating revenue but which may have significant positive effects on the environment. The fiscal character of these taxes should be emphasized and distinguished from the regulatory character of incentive environmental taxes. In addition, there is no functional equivalence between fiscal environmental taxes and direct regulation. There is, however, a functional equivalence between fiscal environmental taxes and other fiscal taxes, such as income tax or VAT.

There is considerable imprecision in the identification of tax measures according to the impact on the environment because it could be argued that, in effect, all tax provisions have an effect on the environment. However, the effects of the tax on the environment may be difficult to verify. Thus the scope of fiscal environmental taxes often has to be determined on the basis of hypothetical effects. In practice, fiscal environmental taxes are not motivated by environmental reasons, such as taxes on energy and motor transport. Road tolls may also be included in this category because their primary goal has usually been fiscal, even though they may have beneficial impacts on the environment. The beneficial effects of environmental taxes are by no means certain in all circumstances. For instance, even though high taxes on motor vehicles discourage the purchase of vehicles relative to other goods, such taxes may also entail incentives to keep older cars in service. This may countervail the effects of lower sales of new cars, as older cars usually use more fuel, have less cleaning devices and thus pollute more. In spite of this, motor vehicle taxes have commonly been perceived as fiscal environmental taxes.

2.4 AN INSTRUMENTAL APPROACH TO ENVIRONMENTAL TAXES

Product taxes are a common form of practically applied environmental taxes.[18] Traditional product taxes have been classified as environmental taxes which are based on the product itself, or rather on the weight, value or the volume of the product. Thus, taxes on disposable items and lubricating oils, for example, belong to this group of taxes. When the product tax is based on environmentally detrimental characteristics, for instance, on the carbon or sulphur content of fuels, it is called a substance-related product tax.

Most of the substance-related product taxes are special in the sense that the environmental tax is directed only at individual products which contain harmful substances. For instance, a tax on nutrients may be directed at fertilizers, but not at the items used in laundering, although they may also contain nutrients, in particular phosphorous. In addition, taxes on cadmium may be implemented as special substance-related taxes, separately from batteries and/or fertilizers. On the contrary, the CFC tax may represent a so-called general substance-related product tax when it is directed, in principle, at all products which contain halons and CFCs. The general substance-related nature is best revealed in the tax treatment of imported products, in which case the tax is imposed on all products if any ozone-depleting chemical was used as an input in the manufacture or production of the products. A general substance-related product tax may also be a tax on chlorinated solvents.

Another important classification is the distinction between *ad quantum* or specific and *ad valorem* or value-based taxes. With an *ad quantum* tax the rate is expressed as a certain amount per physical unit of the products or other tax objects involved and it does not vary with the price of the taxed object.[19] For instance, if the tax is determined by the weight, volume or the content of harmful substances, it is a specific tax. With an *ad valorem* tax the rate is expressed as a certain percentage of the price, and varies with the price. Overwhelmingly, the largest part of incentive, financing and fiscal environmental taxes applied in western Europe are specific taxes.

A large share of environmental taxes have been implemented as tax differentiations. Opschoor and Vos (1989) have defined a tax differentiation as an arrangement which leads to more favourable prices for environmentally friendly products. However, this definition covers only one type of tax differentiation, that offering a price advantage. Another type of tax differentiation is the cost-adjusted tax differentiation. In this case the purpose is not to offer a price advantage in the market for products which are more environmentally friendly, but rather to guarantee the same price for different qualities of products. For instance, the tax differentiation between reformulated and regular petrol in Finland represents this type of differentiation. Tax differentiations usually depend on the technical characteristics of the product. An alternative tax differentiation approach has been adopted in Denmark, where a reduction in the excise duty on petrol distributed by petrol stations meeting more stringent standards of equipment and operation has been applied. The purpose of these standards has been to speed up investment aimed at protecting soil and groundwater from leaks from underground tanks.

Waste taxes can be divided in at least two different ways. First, waste taxes can be classified as general and specific taxes. General taxes are directed at all wastes, if not otherwise stated. A waste tax directed only at chemical waste is a clear example of a specific waste tax. Second, waste taxes can be divided into uniform and differentiated taxes. This distinction is made regarding the differentiation of tax rates according to waste types or according to the use of wastes.

Economists have commonly suggested that effluent taxes would be the best way to implement environmental taxes. However, effluent taxes are a rarely applied form of environmental taxes, at least in western Europe. This feature is due to the fact that in general effluent taxes may be limited to stationary sources. Moreover, non-point sources of pollution, like nitrate leaching, cannot accurately be monitored on a widespread basis at realistic cost, which makes the application of an effluent tax infeasible. On the other hand, the polluting inputs, like nitrogenous fertilizers, can be taxed at moderate costs.[20] Effluent taxes can be defined as taxes paid on discharges into the environment. They are based on the quantity and/or quality of discharged pollutants. First, these taxes can be divided into two categories: taxes on air pollution emissions and those on water pollution emissions. Second, they are classified into one-pollutant and multi-pollutant taxes.

High monitoring costs would make it impossible to levy an effluent tax according to measured emissions by each polluter. Therefore, taxes based on measured emissions are directed only at the largest producers. Such an arrangement needs complementary devices, otherwise the effluent tax may create a threshold effect: there will be an incentive to split the production into two or more plants to avoid the tax burden.[21] Two solutions have been applied to this regulatory problem. First, the effluent tax can be structured as a redistributive environmental tax. Second, it is possible to levy table-based taxes on smaller plants, which are not based on actual monitoring, but rather on the expected or average level of the discharges. This solution is used in some water effluent tax laws.

Noise-related landing taxes are usually differentiated so that aeroplanes are classified into different 'noise classes'. Although landing taxes rest on similar principles in different countries they differ considerably in detail. For instance, aircraft noise taxes on landings may be differentiated according to time of day. This can be called 'a time-differentiated environmental tax'. In some countries the weight of the aeroplanes constitutes part of the tax base.

2.5 RELATIONSHIP BETWEEN ENVIRONMENTAL TAXES AND OTHER INSTRUMENTS IN ENVIRONMENTAL POLICY

The distinction between independent and complementary environmental taxes, which are incentive in nature, is the starting point when examining the different functions of taxes in relation to direct regulation and other policy instruments. In the case of independent taxes, environmental policy is based solely or at least mainly on the incentive environmental tax. In contrast, environmental taxes are called 'complementary taxes' when they are used as an adjunct, in particular, to direct regulation. There have been various general descriptions of complementary taxes: they raise revenues for financing environmental measures, they may provide incentives to better implement the associated regulatory instruments, they may have a possible impact on technical innovation and finally they may precede adjustments of existing regulation or new regulation.[22]

A quite common view has been that the present situation is characterized by the prevalence of mixed systems, in which environmental taxes are only complementary tools to regulatory instruments.[23] However, it has been claimed that this point of view understates the independence of environmental taxes in environmental policy. First, it should be noted that areas such as energy conservation are very difficult to regulate by conventional regulatory instruments. Second, incentive waste taxes are an independent aspect of waste management policy: the possibility to restrict the amount of waste entering waste sites is almost nil using regulatory instruments. Finally, if the purpose of the tax is to reduce, not to prohibit, the use of goods, an environmental tax is a much more viable tool than direct regulation. Hence, taxes on carrier bags and disposable items, for example, have in practice also been independent rather than complementary tools in environmental policy.

According to Stavins and Whitehead (1992), it would be most practical to apply environmental taxes to such problems where environmental policy instruments are not yet in place. This would minimize economic disruptions and reduce the chance of regulations working at cross-purposes. However, environmental taxes are often applied in conjunction with direct regulation in practice. Even though Stavins and Whitehead's concern over coordination problems has to be taken seriously, it does not mean that environmental taxes would be unnecessary in those policy fields where, for instance, direct regulation is in force. We should be pragmatic: regulation has to be evaluated case by case, not by adopting *a priori* the attitude that only independent instruments should be applied.

Incentive environmental taxes complementary to direct regulation are divided here into two groups: reinforcing and preparatory environmental taxes.[24] The purpose of reinforcing environmental taxes is by definition to reinforce direct regulation.[25] Within this context it has also been noted that environmental taxes are applied on the top of direct regulation.[26] In other words, the environmental tax and direct regulation are directed at the same goal and the function of the tax is to provide an incentive to reduce emissions below a regulated emission level.[27]

Preparatory environmental taxes are used to speed up a forthcoming direct regulation. For instance, environmental differentiation of the annual vehicle tax, started in Germany in 1985/86 and declined until it was abolished in the early 1990s, when all new large and medium-sized cars had to meet specified air pollution standards. Moreover, Denmark has applied a reduction in the rate of excise duty on petrol distributed by petrol stations meeting more stringent standards of equipment and operation. The purpose of the standards was to speed up investment aimed at protecting soil and groundwater, and they were made compulsory on 1 January 2005.

Preparatory environmental taxes can be divided into two groups. First, pure preparatory taxes are those environmental taxes which are removed when the new regulation comes into force. Council decisions authorizing the application of differentiated rates of excise duties are often those where the authorization ceases when the regulations become compulsory. Second, a preparatory environmental tax can also continue to be in force after the new direct regulation has been introduced. In other words, this is usually a question of a change in the complementary nature of the environmental tax, and the preparatory tax becomes a reinforcing tax.

Moreover, there are also combinations of environmental taxes and other economic instruments; they are called mixed-type economic instruments. In practice, two such systems have been applied; tax refund systems and redistributive environmental taxes. In the case of a tax refund system, the deposit is levied in the form of tax, whereas the refund is paid in a similar fashion as in a regular deposit refund system. Tax refund systems are applied, for example, on car hulks and batteries.[28] In a redistributive environmental tax system at least part of the tax is refunded to the taxpayers affected by the tax, as in the Swedish emission charge on nitrogen oxides.[29]

NOTES

1   See Pittevils (1996), 203.
2   See Määttä (2003), 175 ff.
3   See OECD (1994), 56.
4   See Opschoor and Vos (1989), 15.
5   See Määttä (1997), 197 ff.
6   See COM(97) 9 final, 3–4.
7   See Messere (1993), 453.
8   See Vos (1994), 15, fn. 11. See De Grauwe (1993), 6.
9   See Opschoor and Vos (1989), 67.
10 See COM(97) 9 final, 8.
11 See OECD (1994), 57 ff.
12 See Pezzey (1992), 989–990.
13 See Nichols (1984), 167, chapter 2, fn. 2.
14 See SOU 1990:59, 461, and Deketelaere (1993), 50.
15 See de Savornin Lohman (1994), 62–63.
16 See SOU 1990:59, 461, and Deketelaere (1993), 50.
17 See for example Huppes and Kagan (1989), 220.
18 See Määttä (1997), 74 ff.
19 See Cnossen (1977), 104–105, and (1992), 128.
20 See Vollebergh (1994), 1 ff, on the reasons why environmental taxes have not been implemented as effluent taxes.
21 See SOU 1989:35, 421, and SOU 1989:83, 223 ff.
22 See Opschoor and Vos (1989), 120, and OECD (1991), 12–13.
23 See OECD (1980), 15, OECD (1985), 189, Hahn (1989), 50, OECD (1993), 10–11, and Driesen (2003), 51 ff.
24 Määttä (1997), 71–73.
25 See OECD (1991), 12, and OECD (1993), 10–11.
26 See Oates (1994), 114.
27 See Gale and Barg (1995), 24.
28 See OECD (1991), 13.
29 See SOU 1989:83, 223 ff, and Olivecrona (1995), 163 ff.

3. The Fallacy of the Buchanan–Tullock Theorem

3.1 PRELIMINARY CONSIDERATIONS

A number of economists have recommended – particularly before environmental taxes were applied on a wider scale – the introduction of environmental taxes on the basis of theoretical economic analysis to provide proper incentives for reducing polluting activities to a desirable level. Until the mid-1980s, politicians and bureaucrats in western Europe favoured direct regulation. This situation has been described by Theeuwes (1991) as a paradox in environmental policy.[1]

How can we account for the paradox? According to the Buchanan–Tullock theorem the answer is that polluters' profits were usually higher in the case of regulatory instruments. Thus, it is in their interest to pressure politicians to work with regulatory instruments rather than environmental taxes. In addition, grandfather clauses in direct regulation make it possible to create entry barriers for new firms, which increase the profits of existing firms. Through grandfather clauses new sources of pollution are regulated more stringently than existing sources.[2] According to Buchanan and Tullock (1975), 'Observed quotas reflect the political power of regulatees'.[3]

With respect to the theorem, there is a need for an analysis of the distributional effects of policies if we are to understand why they have not been adopted. For instance, the direct short-term effects of industrial pollution control policies are concentrated on the affected firms. These effects may form a political cost and thus a stumbling block to the implementation of environmental taxes.[4] Potential distributional 'losers' may be motivated to lobby against measures which would adversely affect their interests, and policy-makers may be concerned about undertaking measures which impose a heavy burden on particular sectors of society. The same holds for subsidy reforms, where attempts are made to remove environmentally detrimental subsidies.[5]

The Buchanan–Tullock theorem is supported to some extent by the fact that in certain cases the resistance of the target groups, such as industry and agriculture, has been a crucial obstacle to the introduction of environmental taxes.[6] Within this context, Opschoor and Vos (1989) have stated that firms prefer direct regulation because taxes might be added to compliance costs; firms often assume that they have more influence on direct regulation, via negotiations, and implementation of new regulations takes a long time because of the negotiations. There are some concrete instances in this. One obstacle in the introduction of air effluent taxes has been the strong opposition from powerful lobbies such as the petroleum industry;[7] airline companies have strongly opposed aircraft noise charges at the national and international levels; in Denmark, a tax on fertilizers was proposed as early as 1984, but was postponed due to massive protests from the agricultural sector; the adoption of a fertilizer tax has also been very difficult in other countries. This resistance is understandable because environmental taxes often create an additional financial burden, a tax bill for polluters, compared with regulatory instruments. Some empirical evidence on this issue suggests that the additional tax burden can be substantial. At a general level, it has been suggested that out-of-pocket costs of achieving a particular emission level at source may easily be doubled by tax payments.[8]

An issue which is not directly related to the Buchanan–Tullock theorem but which is worth mentioning is that bureaucrats may significantly influence the form and content of the legislation. This ability arises simply from their key role in policy-making. For a long time, environmental authorities were thought to be opposed to the introduction of environmental taxes. One explanation for resistance to environmental taxes has been the self-interest of the environmental bureaucracy, whose work might be threatened by such tax approaches. Another explanation for the resistance has been that reliance on direct regulation reflects the legal training of most legislators: lawyers are used to thinking in terms of sharply defined rights and obligations, enforced by the courts, and not in terms of the economic incentives that economists find natural. The Buchanan–Tullock theorem has been criticized in various ways.[9] The aim here is not to give an exhaustive presentation of this criticism but to concentrate on the issues which are relevant to environmental tax policy in practice in western Europe.

3.2 THE IDEA BEHIND THE THEOREM IS QUESTIONABLE

First, the underlying question behind the theorem has to be examined. It can be crystallized briefly in the following way: why have not environmental taxes been adopted despite the fact that economists have recommended the application of these instruments? From the point of view of the expanding environmental tax policy since the mid-1980s, the question itself is misleading,[10] although it must be admitted that in some western European countries environmental tax policy is still currently almost in the same position it occupied in the 1970s, when the theorem was presented. From this perspective, the question should be restated as: why have environmental taxes been introduced since the mid-1980s at a significantly greater rate than before and why is the expansion of environmental tax policy limited to only a few countries?

The question also needs to be elaborated from another point of view. That is to say that the attitude of economists has changed largely from regulation optimism over environmental taxes to pragmatism in this issue. Characteristic of regulation optimism has been the belief in the theoretical advantages of environmental taxes over direct regulation and therefore environmental taxes are usually, according to the supporters of this view, more appropriate instruments of environmental policy. The supporters of pragmatism, however, are more reserved about this conclusion and stress practical aspects and the heterogeneity and multiplicity of environmental problems; that is, a convergence has taken place between actual environmental tax policy and the views of economists. No paradox in environmental policy exists any longer, at least in the sense that Buchanan and Tullock described it in the mid-1970s.

3.3 VARIOUS POLLUTERS AND INTEREST GROUPS

One source of criticism of the theorem is that polluters' attitudes to environmental taxes may be contradictory.[11] The German water effluent tax offers a good example of this. Some industries actually supported the water effluent tax. The two main sources of support were the newer plants with novel waste-saving production processes and the latest pollution control technology, and those older plants with recently installed pollution control equipment.[12] They believed their taxes would be relatively smaller, thus giving them a competitive edge over industrial facilities with less up-to-date equipment.

The preference for direct regulation over taxes depends among other things on the amount of power that particular interest groups have, and how this power is wielded in the political process.[13] Two opposite cases may highlight this issue. For instance, one important obstacle to air pollution taxes has been the strong opposition of powerful lobbies, such as the petroleum industry. On the other hand, the Italian plastic bag tax has been considered easy to introduce because of the weakness of the plastic bag producers' lobby.[14]

More generally, according to Andersen (1995) environmental taxes have often been applied on the basis of the principle of least political resistance. For instance, there is a bias towards the taxation of households because they are a target group poorly organized to lobby for their interests. In addition, environmental taxes are addressed to smaller rather than larger polluters, often granting the latter substantial relief. Related to this issue is the belief that industry initially opposed the idea of any environmental tax system, but as political support for the system gained momentum opposition shifted to implementation issues, such as the criteria for setting the level of taxes, and the dates when the system would take effect.[15]

On the other hand, it has been noted that relations between governments and industry have changed from the confrontational attitudes of the early 1970s to a cooperative approach. This approach is also emphasized in the OECD (1991) guidelines concerning the application of economic instruments, which recommend that adequate information should be given to the target groups about any new instrument. Consultation with target groups should – as far as possible – be involved with the execution of the instruments.[16] A disadvantage of consulting with target groups is, however, that environmental taxes will become more vulnerable to regulatory capture, a phenomenon which has usually been associated with direct regulation. Briefly, this means that regulators act in the interest of target groups rather than in the public interest.[17]

3.4 DIFFERENT WAYS OF IMPLEMENTING ENVIRONMENTAL TAXES

The Buchanan–Tullock theorem has also been criticized in that within particular classes of instruments there is a great deal of variation in their performance. Thus, while the theorem explains why regulatory instruments are chosen over an idealized form of environmental taxes, it does little to help explain the wide variety of instruments that are observed in practice.[18] In other words, the preference for direct regulation over taxes crucially depends on the precise nature of the instruments being compared.

To counterbalance this criticism, it should be mentioned that Buchanan and Tullock (1975) took this aspect into account in their article presenting the theorem when they noted that: '(f)or economists who continue to support the penalty tax alternative, the analysis suggests that they had best become good Wicksellians and begin to search out and invent new institutional arrangements that will make the penalty tax acceptable to those who are primarily affected'. In other words, Buchanan and Tullock demanded the development of legitimacy strategies. Thus, by analysing the factors behind the emergence of an environmental tax policy it is possible to determine which kinds of arrangements – called legitimacy strategies – make environmental taxes acceptable to the target groups as well as to the public. In this section, some legitimacy strategies are outlined.

Redistributive environmental taxes are one way to alleviate resistance to environmental taxes.[19] It is characteristic of these taxes that tax proceeds are refunded to those liable to pay tax, for example, in the form of subsidies to environmental protection investments. An example of this is the Swedish nitrogen oxides' charge. According to Olivecrona (1995), the fact that the charge is refunded and thereby only has an environmental purpose has facilitated its acceptance. However, redistributive taxes have rarely been applied and, thus, the importance of this legitimacy strategy has not been great.[20]

One consideration which has not been taken into account – at least explicitly – in the Buchanan–Tullock theorem is that environmental taxes are not implemented in a 'tax vacuum'. For instance, selective revenue recycling may improve the acceptability of new environmental taxes in the target group. In the case of selective revenue recycling, the introduction of environmental taxes or the raising of tax levels is done without changing the amount of revenue collected from a certain group of taxpayers. Cnossen and Vollebergh (1992) have referred to this strategy by stating 'that considerably more can be done in high-excise countries in restructuring the fuel excise system without increasing revenue yields or average fuel prices'. More generally, it has been contended that an extensive package involving adjustments of both taxes and environmental policy can neutralize the blocking power of interest groups.[21]

This legitimacy strategy has been of greater importance than the implementation of environmental taxes as redistributive taxes. For instance, coinciding with the introduction of the Danish pesticides tax at the beginning of 1996, the property tax levied on agricultural holdings and holdings used for market gardening, nurseries or fruit-growing was reduced. The idea was that the reduction would correspond to the added revenue from the pesticides tax. The introduction of a carbon tax on diesel fuel oils as well as on light and heavy fuel oil in Denmark is also a good example of selective revenue recycling. The tax rates of these fuel oils remained the same after the carbon tax was implemented, which meant that the rate of basic excise tax was reduced by the same amount as the carbon tax rate.[22]

General revenue recycling should not be forgotten within this context either. It implies the introduction of environmental taxes or the increase in their levels without changing total revenues, and without targeting the reduction of other taxes to the target groups of the environmental taxes. Some countries have followed this approach with income tax reduction financed partly by the proceeds from environmental taxes. In the Netherlands, the rate of VAT has been reduced to counterbalance increased proceeds from environmental taxes.

Both redistributive environmental taxes and selective revenue recycling are legitimacy strategies by which the financial burden is mitigated in the groups targeted by environmental taxes. More generally, all measures which can reduce the financial burden of the target groups without affecting the environmental effectiveness and efficiency properties of environmental taxes may be regarded as proper legitimacy strategies. Progressive implementation of the tax rate, that is by originally setting the tax rate at the low level and thereafter gradually increasing it to the target level, at which the tax is assumed to achieve its goals, offers an example of such a strategy. At the same time, it is a means of mitigating the adjustment costs of a new instrument.[23] A progressive timetable in setting tax rates may be appropriate, in particular, regarding those taxes which create a heavy economic burden for polluters. In short, stiff policy measures will bring about fundamental changes in economic institutions and induce transition problems. Low environmental tax rates can provide some evidence of how these taxes affect economic activity while immediate enactment of a high-rate environmental tax would entail a substantial policy risk.[24] Similar functions are served by a delay in implementation, which means the lengthening of the time lag before the new tax is implemented. The German water effluent tax offers an example of this strategy: the system was announced in 1976 but not implemented until 1981.

There are several ways of bringing about the progressive implementation of environmental taxes other than gradually setting the tax rate at higher levels. First, it is possible to start with some products or pollutants and later extend the tax base to cover others. This type of object-related progressive implementation was applied when the Norwegian carbon tax was introduced. Second, environmental tax may be applied in the first stage only to some actors in the economy and later it may be extended to cover all polluters. Such taxpayer-related progressive implementation was applied when the Danish carbon tax was introduced. Third, threshold-related progressive implementation may be applied. The Danish sulphur tax offers an example of this: the tax threshold of fuel oil was 0.4 per cent sulphur in 1996, but it decreased until it reached zero in 2000. Finally, regionally related progressive implementation was applied when the German water effluent tax was introduced: the tax was introduced in 1981 in only three states, but two years later it was extended to cover all states.

It has also been claimed that earmarking proceeds from environmental taxes offers an advantage as it may increase popular support for a new tax since it increases the transparency of the linkage between the tax and the environmental objective.[25] In other words, the earmarking of tax proceeds can be used as a legitimacy strategy in environmental taxation. This claim is to some degree also supported by the experience of various countries. For instance, in Sweden the political opposition to taxes on fertilizers and pesticides is said to have been reduced because money collected was placed initially in a special fund to help overcome the pollution problem.[26] In a similar way, the Dutch water effluent tax has been accepted politically, because it was regarded as an equitable way of financing the construction of sewers and treatment facilities.[27] Some polling data have also shown that public acceptance of environmental taxes is enhanced by allocating their revenues to environmental projects.[28]

On the other hand, earmarking is not of great importance. In practice, financing environmental taxes of minor fiscal significance have been earmarked. Moreover, the earmarking of tax proceeds may not be an unambiguously appropriate way to legitimate environmental taxes. For instance, the earmarking of taxes for specific purposes may inhibit any offsetting reductions in distortionary taxes, such as income taxes.[29] Against this background, it has been more effective not to earmark environmental taxes in environmental protection or other government expenditures but to introduce them in a revenue-neutral way to reduce distortionary taxes. In addition, the Tinbergen rule should be borne in mind here, that is for every goal a different instrument has to be chosen.[30]

3.5 GRANDFATHER CLAUSES

Finally, another critical point in the Buchanan–Tullock theorem must be briefly analysed: new sources of pollution are regulated more stringently than existing sources under direct regulation. These grandfather clauses enable the creation of entry barriers for new firms, and thereby increase the profits of the existing firms. This has also been seen as an expression of the political power of existing firms.[31] On this basis, the application of economic instruments, such as environmental taxes which reduce the role of regulatory procedures and thus facilitate market entry, has been recommended. However, two critical comments should be presented regarding the above argumentation.

On the one hand, there are good reasons to enact grandfather clauses in legislation concerning regulatory instruments. The arrangement is quite often based on considerations of cost-effectiveness in the reduction of pollution. It is even somewhat paradoxical that some of the literature concerning environmental taxes justifies the need to consider the high costs of pollution reduction in existing plants. Therefore, for reasons of cost-effectiveness, for example, the application of a progressive time schedule in setting the environmental tax rate has been recommended.[32] Grandfather clauses serve a similar function in direct regulation, but these clauses are often condemned as inappropriate. On the other hand, grandfather clauses have sometimes been applied in environmental tax laws. One example is the Danish Sulphur Charge Act, which was introduced at the beginning of 1996. A special reimbursement is applied to coal used in certain high energy-consuming boilers and furnaces during a maximum transition period of 20 years in order to avoid an excessive sulphur tax burden on certain processes. Moreover, effluent taxes are sometimes applied only to new effluent sources or to levels of discharge exceeding those current at the time the system is introduced.[33]

NOTES

1   See Määttä (1997), 129 ff.
2   On the subject of grandfather clauses, see Ogus (1994), 169.
3   See Buchanan and Tullock (1975), 139 ff, and Faure and Ubachs (2003), 41–44.
4   See Dewees (1983), 53–54, and De Grauwe (1993), 28.
5   Runge and Jones (1996), 20.
6   See SOU 1989:21, 190.
7   See OECD (1988), 54.
8   Bohm and Russell (1985), 417-418, and Tietenberg (1990), 25.
9   See Coelho (1976), 976–978, Main and Baird (1976), 979–980, and Yohe (1976), 981–982. See the reply to this criticism in Buchanan and Tullock (1976), 983–984.
10 See Hahn (1990), 22.
11 See De Clercq (1996), 63.
12 Brown and Johnson (1984), 932.
13 Hahn (1990), 23.
14 International Fiscal Association (1995), 165.
15 Brown and Johnson (1984), 932.
16 See De Clercq (1996), 64, and Ekins (1996), 24.
17 See Ogus (1994), 57–58.
18 Hahn (1989), 53.
19 See Andersen (1994), 294 ff, and Smith (1995), 91–92.
20 See Marquand (1981), 157–160.
21 Bohm (1994), 86.
22 See TemaNord 1996:568, 75.
23 See OECD (1991), 20.
24 Poterba (1993), 61–62.

25 See Smith (1992), 38–39, OECD (1993), 102, Andersen (1994), 210, and Paulus (1995), 65.
26 OECD (1989), 158.
27 Huppes and Kagan (1989), 220.
28 Bregha and Moffet (1995), 355.
29 See von Weitzäcker and Jesinghaus (1992), 62.
30 See Smith (1997), 29–32, and Spackman (1997), 49–51 on the appropriateness of the earmarking of proceeds from environmental taxes.
31 See Hahn (1990), 27–28.
32 See Medhurst (1993), 45.
33 Ogus (1994), 254.

4. Regulatory and Fiscal Taxes: Theoretical Considerations

4.1 PRELIMINARY CONSIDERATIONS

The discussion concerning direct and indirect taxes or personal and *in rem* taxes is familiar to taxation researchers. Little attention, however, has been paid to the distinction between fiscal and regulatory taxes, even though this distinction is currently especially worth studying.[1]

The purpose of this chapter is to create a conceptual framework for the discussion concerning regulatory taxes. At the same time, the aim is to analyse the usefulness of the concept 'regulatory tax' both *a fortiori*, when regulatory tax laws are designed and implemented, and a posteriori, when these laws are interpreted.

The central question running through all these issues is whether to apply the continuity principle, that is the same 'rules of the game' for regulatory taxes as those applied to conventional fiscal taxes, or whether to give special weight to the regulatory character of taxes concerned. According to the continuity principle, a new legal institution can be integrated into the legal system without preserving its special character and this new legal institution is actually treated in terms of the old. For regulatory taxes, the continuity principle would mean them being treated in exactly the same way as corresponding taxes such as fiscal duties, for instance, when the prohibition of discriminatory taxation under EU law is at issue. In other words, the legal form of the institution would be crucial to any examination of its legal consequences.

Another option is that a new legal institution maintains its special character at least to some extent when it is integrated into the existing legal system. With respect to regulatory taxes, this would mean that they would not be treated in exactly the same way as corresponding fiscal taxes; for example, when the prohibition of retroactive legislation is assessed. The objectives of the institution, and not only its legal form, would determine the legal consequences of regulatory taxes.

4.2 THE NEED FOR THE CONCEPT OF 'REGULATORY TAX'

The need for the concept of a regulatory tax may be justified on similar grounds as the use of the concept 'tax expenditure'.[2] Regulatory taxes by definition serve ends which are similar in nature to those served by direct regulation. This means that a given policy regulation can be structured by using either regulatory taxes or direct regulation to meet the chosen target. Consequently, because regulatory taxes are a route for governments to pursue their policy, they should be subject to similar evaluation and control mechanisms that are used for policy-making provided by direct regulation or other policy instruments.

We should also recall the criticism directed at policy-makers who fail to recognize that tax expenditures exist and understand that they were essentially spending programmes;[3] the same threat is present in regulatory tax policy. If regulatory taxes are not evaluated by similar techniques and criteria as other regulatory policy instruments, the risk remains that these taxes will be regarded in the same light as fiscal taxes. Nevertheless, the criteria for evaluating regulatory taxes differ considerably from those for other taxes. For instance, if regulatory taxes are regarded solely as revenue-generating taxes, there is a great danger of concluding that these taxes are very costly to administer in relation to their yield and that the tax should be removed in spite of the fact that they are primarily regulatory policy instruments. In addition, a review of regulatory policy will be more effective if all the different methods of government intervention are taken into account,[4] and the proper use of a regulatory tax concept may facilitate this task.

The general arguments that the taxpayer should, as much as possible, be able to clearly see what is taxed, and understand the purpose intended by the choice of a particular form of tax, also support the concept 'regulatory tax'.[5] In other words, the proper use of the concept of regulatory tax is compatible with the transparency principle. The other side of the coin is, however, that the legislator may benefit from shifts in attitudes on regulatory issues, and use these shifts as the basis for labelling taxes regulatory taxes, although they are far from instruments serving similar ends as direct regulation.[6] The explicit and actual goals of legislation may deviate from each other in this case. The explicit goals are expressed openly in the preparatory drafts of legislation, but they do not necessarily correspond to the actual goals of the legislation. Consequently, the concept of a regulatory tax causes confusion rather than clarifying the purpose of the tax. The use of 'regulatory tax' can be seen as the use of persuasive definitions and, thus, as a basis for fiscal illusion in these circumstances.

There may also be difficulties in implementing the concept of a regulatory tax, since defining the scope of regulatory taxes is inevitably imprecise. For instance, in the preparatory drafting of regulatory taxes the goals may remain obscure. Certain taxes were originally introduced for fiscal reasons but regulatory considerations have recently become a factor which is taken into account in the structure of the tax in question; in some cases regulatory considerations have been taken into account only by amending part of the tax, and so on.

4.3 FEATURES DISTINGUISHING FISCAL AND REGULATORY TAXES

Taxes can theoretically be divided into fiscal and regulatory taxes.[7] They are traditionally regarded as revenue-raising instruments. Their primary purpose is to generate revenue for the public sector. Value-added and income tax are examples of these fiscal taxes. Currently, however, more and more taxes are being introduced and their primary purpose is to reduce conduct which is contrary to a desired policy goal by making this conduct more expensive. These regulatory taxes have also been defined as taxes which are the functional equivalent of direct regulation.[8] For instance, incentive environmental taxes can be classified as regulatory taxes: they are created in order to guide the behaviour of polluters, whereas their revenues are of secondary importance, if they have any importance at all.

Using Terra's (1988) definition of indirect taxes, regulatory taxes can also be defined in the following way: even if from the economic point of view, a regulatory tax does not guide the conduct of regulatees that are contrary to the intentions of the legislator, the legal character of regulatory taxes still requires the possibility of changing their conduct in accordance with the intentions of the legislator. In indirect taxation the legislator has to ensure that taxpayers have the possibility to take a tax into account in their pricing decisions, whereas with regulatory taxes the legislator must ensure that regulatees have a possibility of considering a tax before deciding on measures which could change their conduct.

From the above-mentioned point of view, the predictability of tax treatment is of great importance in the context of regulatory taxes.[9] Otherwise regulatees will have no opportunity to change their conduct according to the intentions of the legislator and all of the theoretical virtues of these taxes would be eroded. The requirement of predictability has two dimensions. First, the legislator should take predictability into account, and implementation strategies are of great importance here. As a general rule, regulatory taxes should not be implemented at very short notice: delays in implementation are needed to give regulatees sufficient time to take adequate measures.[10] Second, another point of view is the predictability of the decisions made by courts and other judicial bodies. If the decisions of such tribunals are made in an arbitrary way, this is not compatible with the regulatory nature of taxes concerned. When regulatees are not sure about their tax treatment, regulatory taxes become, in effect, fiscal in nature, because the uncertainty of the tax treatment is unlikely to lead regulatees to do anything to change their conduct. In this sense, legal certainty is a necessary, even though insufficient, condition for regulatory taxation to work in the desired manner.[11] The predictability of regulatory tax treatment can be improved, nevertheless, by efficient guidance from authorities, but it must be added that the guidance has its own drawbacks.

The dividing line between fiscal and regulatory taxes is not clear in all cases. For instance, taxes generally have two main objectives. On the one hand, income tax, which can be classified as a fiscal tax, in practice includes regulatory provisions. On the other hand, regulatory taxes often raise revenue. From this point of view, taxes are not usually purely revenue-raising or purely regulatory taxes.[12] Moreover, the distinction between fiscal and regulatory taxes has become obscured because, in particular, incentive environmental taxes are often introduced within the context of tax reforms. In addition, fuel and energy taxes represent another problem connected with the distinction between fiscal and regulatory taxes. Fuel taxes are often mixed taxes incorporating both fiscal and regulatory components. Traditionally, energy products are taxed to raise revenues but more recently regulatory, especially environmentally related, components have been incorporated into these taxes.[13]

An essential feature distinguishing fiscal taxes from regulatory taxes is their primary goal, to generate funds. From this point of view, some further thoughts can be presented on the distinction. It is impossible for a fiscal tax to be a non-revenue-generating tax. It is, however, fully possible for regulatory taxes to be purely regulatory and generate no revenue. Relevant here are redistributive environmental taxes, which only 'recycle' revenues from one polluter to another. In addition, regulatory taxes may be implemented as prohibitory taxes, which would be functionally equivalent to direct prohibitions, and not generate funds.

Regulatory taxes are fiscally paradoxical in the sense that they are instituted to encourage tax minimization, that is to reduce taxable activity.[14] Of course, not all measures to avoid regulatory taxes are acceptable. Therefore, a distinction has to be made between appropriate and inappropriate measures for tax avoidance other than tax evasion. Appropriate measures for tax avoidance are specifically those measures which regulatory taxes encourage and also promote the achievement of policy goals. Inappropriate measures for tax avoidance are such legal measures which reduce the tax burden but do not promote the achievement of policy goals. These measures can take the form of cross-border shopping for taxable products by consumers. In the case of tax evasion, the minimization of the tax burden involves illegal practices, for instance, smuggling taxable products for business purposes. It is possible to intervene against these measures by increasing penalties or by improving the tax control.

The purpose of fiscal taxes is to sustain the tax base, and it is therefore in the interest of the legislator not to bankrupt the taxpayers as a result of taxation. The matter is somewhat different in regulatory taxation. In some cases, the purpose is to erode the tax base completely, as in the case of a tax on environmentally damaging products, which aims at a total shift to the consumption of benign products. In any case, the primary purpose of regulatory taxes is to achieve the desired policy goals, even if it results in such actions as the shutdown of older plants. For this reason and because the threat to close down a factory is unthinkable and not credible in direct regulation, some researchers have even recommended the adoption of regulatory taxes.[15]

A strong emphasis on the fiscal function of fiscal taxes is clearly reflected in the traditional requirements established for excise duties. The principal requirements of such duties have included features like low price elasticity of demand and non-availability of untaxed substitutes for the dutiable goods. Duties on oil, tobacco and alcoholic beverages are seen to meet these criteria well. In contrast, in regulatory taxation the criterion of low price elasticity of demand cannot be imposed. In principle, price elasticity should have no relevance when possible objects for taxation are being examined. This consideration is, however, significant in the sense that, to achieve the policy goals, products which have a low elasticity of demand have to be taxed much more heavily than products with a high elasticity. Nevertheless, actual regulatory tax policy is another matter. For instance, in Belgium, the general philosophy of the Ecotax Law has been that products can only be submitted for environmental taxation if alternative, more environmentally friendly products are available.[16] On the other hand, selective excise taxes have been criticized from a fiscal point of view for not being neutral, that is they discriminate among different items of consumption. A broadly based tax is held to be more appropriate for taxing consumption.[17] From the regulatory point of view this drawback of selective taxes turns out to be an advantage. Selective taxes create opportunities to change the conduct of regulatees.

In summary, given that there are different goals for regulatory and fiscal taxes, the weight of their evaluation criteria must clearly be different. Regarding fiscal taxes, financial efficiency plays a key role, that is the ability to achieve the desired proceeds as efficiently as possible.[18] Regulatory effectiveness, or the capability of the tax to achieve the policy goals established for it as efficiently as possible within a desired time schedule, is an essential feature when evaluating regulatory taxes. Furthermore, the properties of a good tax system deviate, for instance, by the type of the tax and its goals.

4.4 REGULATORY TAXES ARE TAXES BUT...

The commonly held view is that regulatory taxes are indeed, legally speaking, taxes. At a general level, it can be stated that taxes are unrequited payments in which benefits provided by governments to taxpayers are not normally in proportion to their payment. Grabitz and Zacker (1989) have mentioned that taxes in the field of environmental protection need no further definition, since their definition in environmental law is no different from the conventional definition in public finance law. This offers a good instance of the continuity principle.

The legal nature of regulatory taxes does not change as a consequence of their regulatory purpose. Good examples are taxes on tobacco and alcohol, which have traditionally been regarded as taxes, although they are also characterized by a regulatory purpose. Another particular instance is the protective custom duties where the fiscal function is of secondary importance. Finally, in Scandinavian countries, constitutional provisions do not require that the primary objective of the tax be fiscal.

The distinction between penalties and taxes is also important with respect to our topic. As mentioned above, the primary goal of fiscal taxes is to generate funds, whereas the primary goal of regulatory taxes is to change the conduct of taxpayers. Regulatory taxes are functionally closer to penalties than fiscal taxes. Both regulatory taxes and penalties are preventive mechanisms, and the purpose of both appears to be the modification of social conduct which the legislator disapproves of. In contrast, fiscal taxes are not seen as having a preventive function. For instance, income taxes do not aim at reducing participation in the labour force or preventing work, although they may do so in practice, and VAT is never enacted to reduce the consumption of taxable commodities. The purpose of both of these taxes is rather to create a substantial and stable tax base in order to create funds for the public sector.

The convergence between legal institutions can be examined as the distinction between action and constitutive norms. Action norms state what actions must or must not be undertaken. Constitutive norms, on the other hand, neither forbid, require nor permit certain transactions or activities. For instance, regulatory instruments in environmental policy can be classified as action norms, because there is no other choice left to the polluters than to comply or face penalties. Traditional fiscal taxes merely attach certain economic consequences to specific transactions and activities and, thus, they can be classified as constitutive norms. Nevertheless, a rough division of legal norms into action and constitutive norms obscures the fact that norms exist which are directed at changing the behaviour of consumers and producers, although they do not directly forbid, require or permit certain actions. Regulatory taxes belong to this type of norm. Therefore, a distinction can be made between direct and indirect action norms. Regulatory taxes can be classified as indirect action norms, not constitutive norms. For instance, incentive environmental taxes are included in this group of norms because they are a functional equivalent to direct regulation. However, unlike direct regulation, incentive environmental taxes leave polluters free to respond to certain stimuli in a way they themselves consider most beneficial economically. Petrol and motor vehicle taxes, which are primarily intended to raise funds, even though they may have a beneficial impact on the environment, are constitutive norms.

A clear convergence has taken place between legal institutions with a preventive function and to a minor degree there has also been convergence between financing taxes and compensation for damage with respect to a reparative function. An example is the Finnish oil pollution tax, which is levied on imported oil. The proceeds of the tax accrue to the oil protection fund and are mainly used for the procurement of equipment needed for cleaning up oil spills. In the Finnish discussion, it has been suggested that this tax would be a model for complementary schemes in compensating environmental damage. The need for complementary schemes is justified on the grounds that compensation for environmental damage does not guarantee that compensation will be paid, for example, in cases where the liable party is unknown or insolvent. Actually obtaining compensation is by no means certain because claims are hindered by time limitation. Financing environmental taxes would then become a complementary measure for implementing the reparative function to guarantee the provision of compensation.

In summary, legal institutions, which have traditionally been regarded as distinctive from each other, have converged in recent years. It can be claimed that the need for comprehensive policy-making using the most appropriate instruments in each case have created pressures for such development. In some circumstances, these institutions are alternative ways of solving the regulatory problems; in other circumstances, they complement one another.[19] At the same time, new solutions create new problems: in particular, integration or coordination problems may emerge when the range of instruments increases and, for instance, the risk of over-regulation grows.

4.5 STRUCTURES OF FISCAL AND REGULATORY TAXES

The distinguishing features between regulatory and fiscal taxes can be highlighted with regard to the design of these taxes. Concerning the scope of regulatory taxes, the principle of comprehensiveness is paramount. For instance, an incentive environmental tax will be less than comprehensive if all administratively feasible pollution activities are not taxed, and more than comprehensive if activities which do not cause pollution are also taxed. The situation may be quite different with respect to fiscal taxes.

An example may be useful here. Vehicles for off-road use are usually exempted from vehicle taxation. This may have been an expression of the benefit principle: only those who use roads have to pay taxes.[20] With respect to the use of vehicle taxes as a regulatory tool in environmental policy, it makes no difference whether the vehicles are used on the roads or for offroad driving. Regulatory taxes should be levied, in principle, on all these vehicles. On the other hand, if some vehicles do not cause the regulated problems, no regulatory taxes should be levied on them, irrespective of whether they are used on roads or off-road.

The distinction between fiscal and regulatory taxes can also be seen by an examination of the justifications for tax exemptions in VAT and regulatory taxation. In VAT it is considered justified to exempt such activities from the tax which are subsidized to a large degree by the public sector. Health care provides an example of a substantially subsidized sector which has largely remained outside the scope of VAT. Levying VAT on these activities would only lead to reciprocal money transactions.[21] In contrast, exemption of activities subsidized by the public sector from regulatory tax is comparable to exempting those activities from the obligations set in direct regulation. If some sectors were exempted from a regulatory tax it would weaken the environmental effectiveness of the tax unless this exemption were 'offset' by increasing the tax rate of taxable activities. As Cnossen and Vollebergh (1992) stated in their analysis of carbon taxes: 'There should be no exemption from the carbon excise for fuel used by the armed forces, hospitals, homes for [the] aged, scientific and medicinal purposes, or some other worthy goal or institution. The premise is that every burning of fossil fuel by man is potentially climate-threatening.'

In determining tax liability, administrative considerations are central in fiscal taxation. The regulatory option usually preferred is the one yielding the lowest administrative costs. This regulatory standard is also important, of course, with respect to the regulatory taxes. However, when regulatory options are evaluated, their impact on regulatory effectiveness cannot be ignored. For instance, one tax liability option may entail somewhat higher administrative costs than another but would be preferred if it were clearly more compatible with the principle of comprehensiveness.

For administrative reasons simple tax bases are preferable in fiscal taxation. In regulatory taxes the linkage principle has to be taken into account and, thus, the tax should not always be related to the weight or volume of the product, but rather to harmful characteristics of the product. Sometimes it is not even possible to levy a tax on a product; it should be directed at effluents or wastes. However, the transparency principle must also be taken into account: we may require that taxes are related to such attributes that can be monitored and observed. Briefly, the transparency principle has the following dimensions. First, it should be clear to the taxpayers what is and what is not taxable. Second, taxpayers must know how they are taxed: what are the attributes of the tax and what is its level in each case. Third, there must be certainty over who is taxed.[22]

NOTES

1 See Määttä (2002), 155 ff.
2 On tax expenditures, see Surrey (1973), 6 and 28.
3 Surrey and McDaniels (1985), 27.
4 See OECD (1984), 10.
5 Meade (1978), 19.
6 See Buchanan (1967), 134–135.
7 See Surrey (1973), 155, Cnossen (1977), 9 and 155–156, and IEA (1993), 20.
8 See also Surrey and McDaniels (1985), 29.
9 See European Environment Agency (1996), 12.
10 See Pearce and Turner (1990), 115.
11 On legal certainty at a general level, see Aarnio (1986), 3–4.
12 See IEA (1993), 20.
13 See IEA (1993), 15 and Määttä (2003), 175 ff.
14 See Paulus (1995), 4.
15 See White (1976), 113.
16 De Clercq (1996), 48.
17 See Pechman (1987), 201.
18 See Cnossen (1977), 3–4.
19 On these issues, see Shavell (1984), 357 ff.
20 See Cnossen (1977), 9.
21 See SOU 1989:35, 147.
22 Meade (1978), 18–19.

5. Incentive Environmental Taxes

5.1 PRELIMINARY CONSIDERATIONS

An essential feature in the evaluation of incentive environmental taxes is the fact that in a large number of cases there is no empirical evidence about the environmental effectiveness and other properties of the taxes. Thus, in many cases only rough estimates exist about the effects of these environmental taxes. In recent years, however, evidence of environmental effectiveness and other properties of environmental taxes has been growing but proper evaluation studies are still limited in number.[1]

A significant reason for the insufficient data on the effects of environmental taxes is simply that systematic follow-up of environmental taxes has been rare. Individual accounts of the effects of environmental taxes have been made in certain countries, but on the whole, however, lack of research is one reason for the lack of knowledge about the impacts of environmental taxes on the environment. This is emphasized by the fact that environmental taxes are often implemented without forethought to the collection of material needed in the evaluation of the taxes. On the other hand, there are several practical difficulties in evaluating the effects of environmental taxes. An incentive impact may be inconclusive in cases where the environmental tax is applied in conjunction with other environmental policy instruments, as is often the case. In a similar fashion, the effects of the environmental tax component may be difficult to 'isolate' when other taxes directed at the same object exist. For instance, carbon tax constitutes only a part of a large and complex energy tax system, which hinders the analysis of the effects of carbon tax. Changes in external circumstances, like fluctuations in the economic situation, may also cause problems for evaluating environmental taxes. Finally, one reason for the deficient follow-up of some environmental taxes is that they have only been in force a short time. On the other hand, possibilities of drawing more far-reaching conclusions will improve when environmental taxes have been in force for a longer period, and if these taxes are not amended often.

In summary, due to the deficient follow-up of environmental taxes the claims and conclusions made later about different regulations are often 'tentative' in nature. We will discuss the impacts of incentive environmental taxes at the theoretical level and then within the context of designing incentive environmental taxes, that is by analysing those features in incentive environmental taxation which either improve or erode environmental effectiveness as well as the efficiency properties of incentive environmental taxes.

5.2 NATURE OF ENVIRONMENTAL PROBLEMS AND INCENTIVE ENVIRONMENTAL TAXES

The applications of incentive environmental taxes can be highlighted against the environmental problems they are regulating, since in order to construct a viable environmental policy it is necessary to analyse these matters.[2] First, uniformly mixed pollutants should be distinguished from non-uniformly mixed pollutants. In the former, the damage caused by the pollutants is basically irrelevant to the place the emissions are discharged into the environment. The policy can, thus, focus simply on controlling the total weight of emissions. In contrast, for non-uniformly mixed pollutants the policy must be concerned not only with the weight of the emissions entering the environment, but also with the location of the emissions. The concentration of the pollutant in the air, soil and water is significant in this case.

With regard to the carbon tax and CFC tax, from the environmental perspective non-regionally differentiated taxes are justified because they regulate uniformly mixed pollutants. It is problematic that many other environmental taxes are applied as if they regulated uniformly mixed pollutants. This is true of sulphur taxes, taxes on nitrogen oxides and nutrients, which have been imposed as regionally uniform taxes. In other words, they do not vary from place to place in accordance with local differences in damages. On the whole, a peculiar feature of environmental taxes in practice has been their uniformity in many countries.

Another relevant consideration is the distinction between stock and fund pollutants. Stock pollutants are defined as pollutants for which the environment has little or no absorptive capacity and which accumulate over time as emissions entering the environment. Environmental taxes have been levied on such items, for example, as non-biodegradable bottles and other disposable items and heavy metals, like lead in petrol and cadmium in fertilizers and batteries. Fund pollutants are defined as pollutants for which the environment has some absorptive capacity. For those pollutants, as long as the emission rate does not exceed the absorptive capacity, there is no accumulation. Examples of fund pollutants are sulphur dioxide, nitrogen oxide and carbon dioxide emissions, and nutrients which have also been the objects of environmental taxes.

Finally, consideration should be given to the fact that the many environmental taxes relate to pollution problems: air and water quality, chemical risk, waste management and noise. Resource taxes, in this case water taxes and taxes on raw materials, introduced in order to restrict resource usage have not been applied as often.

5.3 IS DIRECT REGULATION SUPERIOR TO INCENTIVE ENVIRONMENTAL TAXES?

One serious problem with incentive environmental taxes is finding the right tax level. The legislator does not know whether polluters will decide to pay a tax or reduce pollution unless the polluters' control costs are known. The settlement of these costs may be a difficult job, because of the asymmetrical information: polluters know these costs but the legislator does not. Therefore, it has quite generally been held that regulatory instruments would be superior to incentive environmental taxes in their environmental effectiveness.[3] However, the issue is not so straightforward.[4]

First, regulatory instruments also may have unpredictable effects on total pollution. An example of this is the provisions regulating the maximum sulphur content in fuels. This does not guarantee that some exactly defined state of the environment would be achieved since, among other things, the demand for fuels can change as can total production or the number of polluters.[5] Against this background, there is not necessarily any significant difference between the environmental effectiveness of a sulphur tax on fuels and provisions regulating the maximum sulphur content in the same fuels.

Second, distinctive legislative techniques are followed by direct regulation and environmental taxes. In the former, flexible norms are often applied. This means that the law in itself does not specifically determine the obligations imposed on polluters, which often results in problems of interpretation. In addition, these instruments are often formed by weighing up conflicting aims: on the one hand, there is the desire to protect the environment and, on the other hand, the question of what polluters can afford. Thus, the environmental effectiveness of direct regulation implemented as flexible norms rests on an indeterminate basis. Another legislative technique is, however, usually followed in environmental taxation. According to the legality principle, the law should contain all essential elements of a tax, such as the rate and base of the tax and provisions concerning tax liability. It seems likely that this property of environmental taxes, in comparison to flexible norms, better promotes the achievement of environmental policy goals.

Third, the uncertain effect of regulatory instruments in the state of the environment is also caused by the fact that these instruments are not necessarily 100 per cent effective. It has been suggested that compliance with direct regulation has to be seen as the result of economic decisions by the target groups based on balancing marginal non-compliance costs with marginal compliance costs. According to this analysis, some optimal rate of compliance exists and, thus, compliance with the direct regulation is not an 'all-or-nothing' decision.[6] In addition, there are views which emphasize that differences exist between tax authorities and environmental regulators in practices regarding enforcement and compliance. There is a rather common view that tax authorities are 'tougher' in this respect.[7] However, the significance of this argument should not be exaggerated: where direct regulation is enacted as flexible norms, environmental authorities have wide discretionary power, whereas the discretion of tax authorities is limited.

Fourth, in some situations the application of environmental taxes may not be warranted, and in others direct regulation may be difficult or impossible to implement. Jacobs (1991) has expressed this point succinctly regarding the latter case when he states that:

> taxes may be more effective than regulations in reaching an environmental target (other than zero) where it is consumers' rather than producers' behaviour which needs to be controlled. Given the number of users of consumer products – for example, paper – it is very difficult to design a regulation which reduces consumption without actually eliminating it altogether. In contrast, by changing its price a tax can change a product's consumption by variable amounts.

More specifically, environmental taxes may be preferable to direct regulation when the aim is to reduce the consumption of, say, disposable products, the generation of waste, or gradually increase the market share of environmentally friendly fuel qualities. If direct regulation was applied in these circumstances it would be over-inclusive, deterring more than the environmental policy goal requires.

The use of preparatory environmental taxes is also worth noting. For instance, if certain legal obligations, due to direct regulation, are to take effect at the beginning of 2010, it would mean that the purchases needed to adjust to the new legislation should be concentrated at the end of 2009. What would happen? The prices of investments would increase and could even lead to problems in fulfilling the new requirements. To avoid this 'congestion' of investments, preparatory environmental taxes could be applied; that is these taxes could be introduced in order to encourage economic actors to invest before the new obligations are implemented. Such preparatory regulation could balance the investments over a longer period as well as level the costs of the investments. This is, of course, appropriate with regard to both environmental effectiveness and cost-effectiveness.

It is also worth noting that environmental problems have changed in character, and are now more often diffuse. In the 1970s and 1980s many of the most acute and concentrated environmental problems were brought under control, partly as a result of direct regulation. It was often a matter of point sources, such as combustion facilities, where the sources and magnitudes of discharge could be identified and measured with a reasonable degree of certainty and exactitude. More diffuse sources, such as traffic and consumption, pose more difficult control problems. A rather commonly held view is that environmental taxes are usually an appropriate instrument in these circumstances.[8] Thus, it is hardly surprising that effluent taxes – directed at point sources – have been rarely applied in practice, and that a large part of environmental taxes is directed at non-point sources, such as traffic and consumption. From this point of view, it is also understandable that many environmental taxes are in practice directed at the final goods, that is products creating waste management problems.

Finally, even though it is difficult to find the right level for environmental taxes, it is not impossible. Economists have often recommended an iterative, trial-and-error process.[9] This process begins by setting the tax rate at an arbitrary level. If it leads to under-inclusive pollution reduction, the tax rate is raised and vice versa. The process continues until the right tax level is found. However, an iterative process has aroused considerable criticism and it is not surprising that this procedure for finding the right tax level has rarely been applied in practice.[10] Two other procedures, however, have been used for this purpose.

First, incentive environmental tax rates have gradually been raised until the target level or the desired impacts on the environment have been achieved; that is a rate-related progressive implementation of environmental taxes. This procedure has been applied, for example, within the context of the German water effluent tax, both when it was introduced in 1981 and when it was reformed in 1990. Similarly, progressive implementation characterizes many of the environmental taxes which have been introduced or restructured in the Danish environmental tax reform which began in 1993.

Another procedure for finding the right tax level and guaranteeing an acceptable state of the environment is to apply mixed systems. In other words, direct regulation can be used as a transitional arrangement before the right level of incentive environmental tax is found. Direct regulation may be kept to a minimum standard and environmental taxes may be used to tighten environmental policies, but only temporarily. In the longer run, however, mixed systems which only rely on this justification lead to over-regulation. One of the policy instruments, either direct regulation or environmental tax, is a binding constraint. On the one hand, if direct regulation constitutes this constraint, environmental tax is *de facto* a fiscal tax, and, on the other hand, if taxes induce polluters to do more than what is required in direct regulation, there is no longer any need for it.[11]

In summary, there is no basis for claiming that direct regulation would be superior to environmental taxes in spite of the difficulties in setting the tax rate at the right level. On the one hand, serious shortcomings also exist in direct regulation concerning environmental effectiveness and, on the other hand, procedures exist which permit an incentive environmental tax be levied at the right level without endangering the state of the environment.

In seeking to find the right tax level, we can ask whether environmental policy goals should be set financially, so that abatement measures would not cost above some amount per kilogram of pollution units. Goal-setting like this is not totally unknown in direct regulation. For instance, when the Finnish regulation on nitrogen oxides was reformed at the turn of the 1990s, an essential benchmark was that technical measures to reduce nitrogen oxide emissions should not cost more than approximately 3000 euros per tonne of nitrogen dioxides. If this kind of goal-setting is followed in environmental policy, environmental taxes would become superior to direct regulation. With the tax on nitrogen oxides, the goal is achieved simply by setting the tax at the level of 3000 euros per tonne of nitrogen dioxides, but with direct regulation, asymmetrical information between regulatees and regulators would make it much more difficult or even impossible to select the required measures, and the costs would fall below the financial target.

Is financial goal-setting solely a theoretical alternative? We think that it is not. As Kneese and Schultze (1975) have pointed out, environmental policy goals are not the simple consequence of how clean we want the environment to be. In establishing goals we are confronted with a set of choices and conflicts between environmental quality and other aspects of living standards. In other words, environmental protection is to a large extent a balancing of different interests. In addition, environmental targets are often set in a rather arbitrary way. Andersen (1995) put this succinctly when he noted that there is no reason why the 1987 Danish pesticides plan requires a 50 per cent reduction of pesticide use, rather than a 30 per cent or 70 per cent reduction. According to Andersen, the chosen target appears to be the outcome of a genuine political process. When environmental policy is developed, we should therefore consider not only alternative instruments and their design, but also the options available for setting the targets of environmental policy.

Another source of criticism of environmental taxes is that they are inappropriate tools for regulating non-uniformly mixed pollutants. This is confirmed by the fact that incentive environmental taxes are often regionally uniform. However, within this context the change in the nature of environmental problems is one factor which must be taken into account.

Global pollutants are currently in the forefront of national and international environmental policies. The search for policy instruments that can make the necessary adjustments and address these problems has brought attention to the potential benefits of using incentive environmental taxes,[12] and it has been emphasized that environmental taxes are likely to be more appropriate for non-spatial problems such as global warming than for local pollution problems. In other words, carbon dioxide, for example, is a good candidate for taxation because it is a uniformly mixed problem source and consequently the damage caused is unrelated to where the emissions are released into the atmosphere, and there is no need for regional differentiation.

Even though uniform incentive environmental taxes ignore spatial considerations, space for their application also exists in this context. Mixed systems, in this case permanent ones, may solve the regulatory problem connected with pollution, which vary significantly from place to place. In a system like this incentive environmental taxes would be applied to encourage a general reduction in pollution, and direct regulation would be instituted to prevent 'hot spots' problems.[13]

5.4 DESIGNING INCENTIVE ENVIRONMENTAL TAXES

5.4.1 Marginal Tax Rate

The basic premise in the economic literature has usually been, for instance, that an effluent tax is levied on each unit of pollution emitted into the air or water. The total payment any source would make to the government could be determined by multiplying the tax rate by the amount of pollution emitted. In this case, the tax is proportional since the ratio of taxes paid on pollution is constant regardless of the pollution level, or the average rate is constant.

With regard to the environmental effectiveness of environmental taxes, the marginal tax rate is crucial. The marginal tax rate is the change in environmental tax paid concerning a change in pollution; for example, in the case of effluent taxes, it is the additional tax which the polluter must pay for each additional unit of pollution. The marginal tax rate can also be expressed in terms of the amount of tax savings to the polluter if pollution is reduced by one unit.

As a general rule, the higher the marginal environmental tax rate is, the greater the incentive to reduce pollution. In this respect, the total tax burden facing the polluter is not a crucial matter, because it is possible that the marginal tax rate is low or zero, even though the tax burden is heavy. The problem of a zero marginal tax rate is a familiar one in effluent taxation: effluent taxes on minor polluters may not be based on the measured effluent, due to high measuring costs, but on table-based taxes. In such cases, the environmental tax paid by smaller plants remains the same regardless of the pollution level, and these polluters have no incentive to reduce pollution. The problem of the zero marginal tax rate has also at times been examined in the context of product-related environmental taxes. For instance, a relief procedure initially applied to Swedish energy and carbon taxes limited the payment of taxes to 1.7 per cent of the firms' sales value of manufactured products. Firms which fell below this provision in fact had a zero marginal tax rate and, thus, no incentive to reduce carbon dioxide emissions and energy consumption.[14]

However, it has usually been the case that the marginal tax rate has been too low to have affected the behaviour of polluters. This default was common particularly in the 1980s. For instance, a water pollution tax and a tax on air pollution in France and a tax on pesticides in Sweden were regarded as environmentally ineffective because of the too low tax level. Carbon taxes both in Finland and the Netherlands were seen as environmentally ineffective due to their low level in the early 1990s. Nevertheless, many environmental taxes have later proven effective from the environmental point of view. Such examples are the Swedish sulphur tax and the nitrogen oxide charge. There has also been evidence that the Swedish fertilizer tax has reduced the use of nitrogen and phosphorous. Moreover, high taxes on disposable packaging in Denmark, Finland and Norway have been viewed as the cause of the large market share of returnable glass in these countries. Taxes on carrier bags in Denmark and Ireland have probably also been effective. In addition, the European Environment Agency stated in 2000 that in general, tax rates in the member states are sufficient for full internationalization of external costs, for giving correct signals to the market, and for establishing a more efficient and equitable fiscal system. Of course, the marginal tax rate is also important for cost-effectiveness. If the tax rate is so low that an incentive environmental tax does not influence the behaviour of polluters, such a tax cannot be legitimated at all by cost-effectiveness.

5.4.2 Incentive Environmental Taxes and Value-Added Tax

According to Article 11(A.2.a.) of Directive 77/338/EEC, '[t]he taxable amount shall include taxes, duties, levies and charges, excluding the value-added tax itself' in VAT. This means that environmental taxes directed at products are usually part of the taxable amount. On the other hand, according to Article 17(2), the main rule is that '[i]n so far as the goods and services are used for the purposes of his taxable transactions, the taxable person shall be entitled to deduct from the tax which he is liable to pay'. This would mean that the environmental tax incorporated into the taxable amount in VAT could also be deducted by those who have the right to deductions.

With regard to environmental taxes directed at final products used by the consumers, such as beverage containers and carrier bags, environmental taxes remain part of the taxable amount in VAT. This should be taken into account in setting the nominal rate of an environmental tax. Consequently, VAT generates the need for a lower nominal environmental tax rate in order to guarantee the achievement of environmental policy goals.

Problems related to VAT emerge in the case of the same environmental tax being directed both at the consumers and producers. Namely, it can be said that the effective tax burden of business is lower in these circumstances than the tax burden of the consumers. This is simply because business has the right to deductions but consumers do not. Regulatory options mitigating or preventing this problem exist: on the one hand, restricting the deductibility of environmental taxes in VAT, and, on the other hand, applying a higher environmental tax rate for business, when an environmental tax is directed both at production and consumption. A third regulatory option would be the alternative applied in the Irish environmental tax on plastic bags. When calculating VAT liability, retailers who account for VAT under a retailer's scheme should simply exclude the plastic bag tax from the turnover figure. Retailers who do not use a retailer's scheme should ensure that the levy is not included in the taxable amount for VAT.

In the first regulatory option, it has previously been common practice in VAT to deny a credit of input tax in relation to certain business purchases which by their nature can easily be appropriated for private use, for example, motor vehicles and motor fuels.[15] In the alternative regulatory model environmental tax in income taxation would be non-deductible.[16]

However, there are difficulties in implementing the non-deductibility of environmental taxes. First, deductibility may offer a tool for controlling and thereby reducing tax fraud. Nevertheless, it is also possible that this deductibility offers an incentive for tax evasion in the sense that there is an inducement to purchase items in the name of the firm although these items are used in practice by the consumer. Preventing misuse of this kind has specifically been the purpose of non-deductibility of motor vehicles and motor fuels in VAT in some countries. Second, administrative problems cannot be avoided if the deductibility of environmental taxes in VAT is prohibited.[17] The non-deductibility option would require that environmental taxes are listed in invoices so that the arrangement is possible in practice.

Another option would be to raise the rate of an environmental tax for those economic agents who have a right to a deduction in VAT. Such an option has been employed in Sweden on real estate taxes, but has not been used with regard to environmental taxes. Apart from being difficult to administer, this regulation involves an incentive to tax arbitrage, particularly in regard to product-related taxes. In other words, the problems would be similar to those facing regionally differentiated product taxes. Thus, this option may be viable only for taxes other than product-related taxes.

To sum up, the procedures which have briefly been analysed involve difficult practical problems and neither of them can be recommended to streamline the tax treatment of consumers and business.

5.4.3 Timetables for Setting the Incentive Tax Rate

Timetables for setting the rates of environmental taxes can be divided into one-phase implementation and multi-phase or progressive implementation.[18] In one-phase implementation the tax rate is set directly at the target level, that is the level at which the tax is assumed to achieve its goals. It is irrelevant that the tax rate may have to be adjusted later. The characteristic feature of multi-phase or progressive implementation is that it begins by setting low tax rates and increasing them until the target level or the desired quantitative response is achieved. In addition, it is possible to delay implementation, to extend the time lag before the tax is put into effect within the context of both of these implementation strategies.

Progressive implementation can be divided into fixed and open procedures. With fixed implementation there is a set schedule for the rates. An open procedure contains no suggestion of an annual increase to a certain level, but only states that possible increases should be considered after reviewing the progress made in implementing national plans. A progressive timetable in setting tax rates may be appropriate in particular for taxes which create a heavy economic burden for polluters. Progressive implementation is a means of preventing rapid increases in financial burdens, and thus mitigates adjustment costs. Moreover, low incentive environmental taxes can provide evidence on how these taxes affect economic activity while immediate enactment of a high-rate tax would entail a substantial policy risk.[19] A progressive timetable may be seen as an alternative to the iterative process in setting the environmental tax rate. For instance, Pezzey (1988) has recommended the use of progressive implementation instead of applying a trial-and-error process. In this strategy we know the direction environmental tax rates will take, which may not be the case in the iterative process.

There is other evidence to support the use of a progressive schedule in setting environmental tax rates. For instance, it has been argued that environmental taxes will fuel inflation.[20] One way of alleviating this impact is to employ progressive implementation.[21] A progressive timetable is also regarded as a means of mitigating undesirable impacts on income distribution.

In addition, in many instances it has been emphasized that it would be more acceptable to introduce an environmental tax, such as the carbon tax, in a gradual manner.[22]

The length of the timescale applied is a difficult regulatory problem not only in relation to the fixed progressive timetable but also with respect to a delay in implementation. This is because the speed with which environmental taxes are introduced can be critical in determining the response adopted by polluters. For instance, it has been suggested that too short a timescale will favour the adoption of end-of-pipe technologies since alternative clean technologies may not immediately be available. It has also been noted that quick implementation may lead to an unjustified increase in the price of de-pollution plants because of a growth in demand. Therefore, a short timescale will erode the technological flexibility *de facto* and thereby the cost-effectiveness of an environmental tax. In addition, it is important that polluters have sufficient time to comply, thus encouraging an innovative response to the environmental tax, that is to promote at least potentially dynamic efficiency. On the other hand, too long a timescale may send the wrong signals to polluters, because it may give the impression that improving the state of the environment need not be a high priority. Uncertainty over future environmental tax policy may also increase because external circumstances may change, among them political attitudes and the relative strength of political groups.[23]

All in all, we need to strike the right balance between a timescale which enables polluters to respond in a way that minimizes short-termism and one which is too long and allows for too many variables. Of course, the timetable for achieving the goals is of great importance. If the goals set have to be achieved at very short notice, the use of a progressive timetable is not possible.

5.4.4 Regional Differentiation of Incentive Environmental Taxes

There is no need for regional differentiation in the case of uniformly mixed pollutants, for example, CFCs and carbon dioxide emissions, because the environmental damage is not dependent on where the pollution source is located. Moreover, the suitability of regionally differentiating taxes on disposable items is also questionable. For non-uniformly mixed pollutants, in contrast, the view is that the policy must also concern itself with the location of the emissions. Thus, there would, in principle, be a need for regional differentiation.

However, there are also several arguments for uniform environmental taxes in the case of non-uniformly mixed pollutants. Uniform taxes are easier to administer. In the case of product taxes, they must be the same for all products throughout the whole country.[24] Otherwise, there will be a margin for tax arbitrage: those offered lower prices would resell to those paying higher prices, thereby cancelling out the gain from regional differentiation. Any chance of controlling the tax arbitrage would be limited.[25] Moreover, in the case of taxes on motor vehicle registration, there would be an incentive to register vehicles where the tax is low if regional differentiation is applied.

In this light, the answer to the regulatory problem of regional differentiation of product-related environmental taxes is not difficult. Even though there is considerable variation in the severity of environmental problems, regional differentiation is simply not feasible and it can be ignored. Nevertheless, regionally differentiated excise duties are not totally unknown in the EU. An example is the Council decision of 18 February 2002 authorizing Portugal to apply a reduced rate of excise duty in the autonomous region of Madeira on locally produced and consumed rum and liqueurs and in the autonomous region of the Azores on locally produced and consumed liqueurs and *eaux-de-vie*. This example shows, however, that regional differentiation of product taxes may be realistic only in specific circumstances.

The regulatory problem is mainly restricted to effluent taxes. Nor have attitudes towards the regional differentiation of effluent taxes been positive in every respect. The first criticism is that a regionally differentiated tax would provide an incentive to firms – in particular for new plants – to move operations from 'dirty' regions to clean regions to avoid paying a higher tax. One way to prevent the degradation of the environment in the cleaner regions is by imposing a uniform tax in all regions.[26]

Second, it is generally held that the 'tax boundaries' will be contested because firms may obtain substantial tax benefits from small changes in boundary lines. Therefore, the competitive neutrality of environmental taxation may suffer; this is a crucial factor determining the acceptability of environmental taxes.

Third, emphasis has been placed on the multidimensional nature of many pollutants, which may argue for a uniform tax. Local circumstances can be taken into account, in this case particularly, through direct regulation. In other words, mixed systems may be used to regulate the problems of 'hot spots'.[27]

Fourth, there is a drawback if regional differentiation is implemented by delegating legislative power to local authorities: an element of discretion is thus introduced into the tax system. This can permit polluters to gain an unjust benefit.[28] In other words, incentive environmental taxes would become the target of the same criticism, regulatory capture, that is usually directed at regulatory instruments. On the other hand, how can we guarantee that the application of incentive environmental taxes is uniform across the country, if local authorities apply environmental tax legislation? Of course, environmental reasons may justify the non-uniform application of the legislation. Otherwise the tools guaranteeing uniform practice are the same as in taxation in general.

Fifth, the delegation of legislative power to local authorities creates pressures to shift the administration of environmental taxes to the environmental authorities, because they have the expertise in dealing with the local circumstances in environmental regulation. On the other hand, they have no expertise in the collection of taxes. Any administrative advantages in linking environmental taxation to other parts of the tax system are also lost.

In summary, for the large portion of incentive environmental taxes, particularly product-related taxes, regional differentiation is only of theoretical interest. In the case of other types of environmental tax, in particular effluent taxes, it is questionable whether regional differentiation of taxes is appropriate.

5.4.5 Tax Relief Under Environmental Taxation: the Carbon Tax Relief Example

The influence of environmental regulation, including environmental taxes, on the competitiveness of firms has divided opinion in the literature.[29] Some have emphasized that environmental regulation leads to a loss of competitiveness because regulation imposes significant costs on firms. Others argue that environmental regulation has positive impacts on international competitiveness. For instance, front-runner advantages have often been a repeated argument.[30] In other words, industry will gain a competitive advantage by early investment in environmental technologies, once they know that target levels of environmental policy will be tightened in the future.[31] In environmental tax policy practice, it appears that the first approach has had more weight.

However, competitive disadvantages depend on many things. First, if the carbon tax paid is insignificant compared to the overall costs of firms, competitive disadvantages are not significant. Second, competitive disadvantages depend on the measures taken in competing countries. Third, the impact of carbon taxes on competitiveness can be offset to some extent by certain domestic measures. For instance, it is possible to apply selective revenue recycling or progressive implementation of a carbon tax. Nevertheless, perhaps the most important measure has been to apply carbon tax relief to maintain the competitiveness of businesses and in order to prevent the relocation effect.[32] Carbon tax relief can be classified according to the targeting procedure of the system, that is how the scope of the tax relief is limited.[33] Three procedures can be outlined: a sector procedure, an energy-intensity procedure and an offset procedure. Tax relief applied in practice are often mixed procedures in the sense that two or all three procedures are applied jointly.

In a sector procedure carbon tax relief is directed at all firms in some specified sector of the economy. In an energy intensity procedure the tax relief is directed towards firms having the highest energy intensity, computed as an approximation of significant costs caused by the carbon tax. Energy intensity can be defined as total energy consumption expenditure measured as a percentage of sales value. It is also possible that so-called ceiling provisions are connected to the energy intensity procedure. This means that no carbon tax is payable if the energy intensity of a firm reaches a certain level. In an offset procedure tax relief is granted to firms which are investing in the reduction of carbon dioxide emissions. In principle, the offset procedure means that instead of paying the full amount of the carbon tax, the polluter can use part of the money for measures taken to reduce carbon dioxide emissions.

From the environmental effectiveness point of view, it is important to note that climatic change is a global problem. The detrimental effects of carbon dioxide emissions are the same regardless of where they are emitted. Therefore, if unilateral measures merely result in the transfer of emissions from one country to another, the aim of preventing climatic change goes unfulfilled.[34] Against this background, the need for and appropriateness of carbon tax relief is dependent on the carbon leakage rate, the amount of carbon dioxide emissions moving abroad due to carbon taxation. The higher the carbon leakage rate is, the more justified it is to apply carbon tax relief if it can prevent the leakage without causing substantial disadvantages in respect of the effects of carbon taxation.

Energy costs usually represent a small fraction of the total costs for most activities within an economy. As far as such activities are concerned, a uniform carbon tax can reduce carbon dioxide emissions effectively. However, energy-intensive industries competing in the world market may be vulnerable to changes in their competitive position. Therefore, carbon tax relief must be restricted to only those sectors in which the economic burden created by a general carbon tax is likely to cause a relocation effect. We would also refer to one condition of the polluter-pays principle that subsidies be allowed if they are selective and restricted to those parts of the economy, such as industries, areas or plants, where severe difficulties would otherwise occur.

Hence, the preliminary recommendation is to limit carbon tax relief to some specified sectors. This limited sector procedure is not, however, unproblematic. First, the energy intensity may vary significantly between firms in these sectors too and in this sense some firms may get tax relief although they do not need it. Second, there may be firms outside these sectors with high energy intensity. Third, the selection of the effected sectors is also a very delicate matter politically.[35] Such sectors may have to be mentioned in the law, which would reduce the external flexibility of the carbon tax with regard to changes in production structures.[36] At first glance, the energy-intensity procedure seems to avoid this problem. However, when this procedure is applied in practice, the sectors benefiting from such a procedure are limited. In this respect, the energy-intensity procedure suffers like the sector procedure from external inflexibility. Finally, an essential problem related to the application of tax relief more generally is asymmetrical information between the regulator and regulatees. The legislator is not certain of the carbon tax level which would cause the relocation effect. Therefore, the legislator has to trust the regulatees to a large extent in this matter.

A crucial issue, in any case, is the overall level of the carbon tax. If the tax rate is low, it is possible that distortion would be minimal even for energy-intensive industries and no tax relief is required. This point of view has been emphasized in some countries: tax relief is needed only after the carbon tax has created a significant cost burden to industry relative to competing countries. However, the danger of such a premise is evident: it excludes any substantial increases in carbon tax rates. On the other hand, a carbon tax with a permanently low tax rate is likely to be environmentally ineffective. In this respect, the issue involves a tax level paradox, a low tax level having no impact on the environment and a high one causing a large-scale relocation effect. The application of carbon tax relief can be seen as a compromise between these two extreme options.

From a cost-effectiveness point of view carbon tax relief may be problematic, because the potential for reducing carbon dioxide emissions from relieved sectors at relatively low costs will not be fully utilized.[37] If no relocation effect exists, obtaining a given reduction in carbon dioxide emissions would require the application of a higher tax to other sectors when tax relief is incorporated into the carbon tax.[38] This is quite clear from the calculations made in connection with the Danish energy tax reform implemented in 1996. It was estimated that the climate policy objectives could be accomplished by a tax rate of DKK 200 per tonne of carbon dioxide, but when tax relief procedures were applied the tax rate should have been DKK 600 per tonne of carbon dioxide on those sectors where no relief was given. Further problems concerning cost-effectiveness emerge from the different marginal tax rates of firms receiving tax relief. In this context the marginal tax rate means the change in carbon tax paid in connection to the change in the amount of carbon dioxide emissions.

The energy-intensity procedure may also cause other unjustified distortions between firms. For instance, the activities of one firm may be comprised solely of an energy-intensive process, but another firm may also engage in other less energy-intensive activities. The first firm will pay less carbon taxes than the latter for the same energy-intensive process when carbon tax relief is related to the total value-added of the firms. An offset procedure is problematic with regard to this issue, if the procedure is based on design provisions, that is provisions which connect the granting of tax relief to some specified technical measures.

Administrative difficulties cannot be avoided if carbon tax relief is applied. A case in point is the potential for tax arbitrage, because some buyers get taxable products at a lower tax rate than others.[39] Moreover, carbon tax relief may encourage speculation through the separation of particularly energy-intensive areas of production into formally independent entities. By means of this procedure a number of firms may attempt to reduce their tax liability. Nevertheless, according to Piacentino (1994) the administrative problems generally connected with the carbon tax relief should not be exaggerated. He refers to the taxation of diesel fuel oil in European countries: even though the tax on the transport sector has often been much higher than in heating, problems have been limited. Empirical evidence shows, however, that administrative considerations cannot be so readily dismissed. For instance, the Danish energy and carbon tax reform instituted at the beginning of 1996, and the Finnish Energy Tax Reform of 1997 introducing tax relief for industry, led to a substantial increase in the number of officials working with excise taxation.

One criticism levelled commonly against carbon tax relief is that the duration is not specified. For instance, it has not been unusual to emphasize the temporary nature of tax relief while connecting its abolition to the measures taken at the international level. The temporary nature of tax relief is also emphasized in the Community Guidelines of the State Aid for Environmental Protection. This refers to the possibility that 'temporary' measures may in effect become permanent due to the difficulty in determining the type of actions other countries would have to take before the country ends the tax relief. The danger that such tax relief may become permanent provides strong grounds for extreme caution in introducing them in the first place.[40]

Some guidelines may also be sought in the polluter-pays principle, especially with respect to the exceptions allowed in this principle. One condition for an exception is that it must be limited to a well-defined time period. One could, therefore, claim that relief from the carbon tax would also have to be temporary, and in addition, not open-ended but limited to precisely defined time periods. This arrangement may have its pros and cons. It improves the predictability of the tax treatment provided that the timetable is also maintained. It is also in the interest of the business community to have the scope for adjusting its operations to new and higher carbon tax rates. However, matters concerning the future are always uncertain. For instance, if the most important competitor countries have taken no measures to reduce carbon dioxide emissions, would there be enough political courage, or even the rationale, to end the tax relief?

Related to the above, the application of tax relief also creates legal uncertainty, which can be reflected as a volatility of carbon taxation. Tax relief is primarily regarded as state aid under EU law. Therefore, uncertainty may exist over the legality of the tax relief. In contrast, because some degree of specificity in determining state aid is required, a uniform, even though low, carbon tax does not include state aid and in this respect it does not create legal uncertainty. Moreover, the granting of tax relief is temporary, a few years at most. In these circumstances, the predictability of the tax treatment is weak, which is not compatible with the regulatory character of a carbon tax. In addition, there is an inherent contradiction in the sense that carbon tax should be as stable as possible while tax relief should be temporary. However, it should be emphasized that the attitude of the European Commission has generally been positive with respect to carbon tax relief. There are many justifications for this. First, it is desirable that energy taxes should be increased to reduce carbon dioxide emissions. Second, the introduction of carbon tax has been regarded as politically impossible in the absence of a tax relief component. Third, tax relief would not be a tool for providing competitive advantages to domestic firms but a tool to prevent competitive disadvantages.

5.4.6 Tax Differentiations

Tax differentiation favouring unleaded petrol has speeded up the consumption of this petrol quality so that in many countries leaded petrol has vanished from the market. This differentiation is based on the principle of price advantage, which leads to more favourable prices for environmentally friendly products. Even though no evident correlation has existed between the tax differential (taking into account VAT) and the market share of unleaded petrol as well, it is obvious that tax differentiation has effectively promoted environmental policy goals.

The incentive impact of the tax differentiation of unleaded petrol has also been connected to the 'conscience effect' of the tax differentiation: tax differentiation has 'signalled' the environmental benefits of unleaded petrol to car owners and has had in this sense an informative function.[41] Furthermore, the general attitude is that an environmental tax which is simple and transparent in design will promote the achievement of environmental policy goals.[42]

Cost-adjusted tax differentiations have in many cases also proved to be environmentally effective instruments.[43] In this case the purpose is not to offer a price advantage in the market for products which are friendlier from an environmental point of view, but rather to guarantee the same price for different qualities of products. This is borne out by the experience of Finland, where reformulated petrol has practically displaced the normal grades, as well as the Swedish environmental classification of petrol tax.

The Portuguese tax differentiation of heavy fuel oil, however, led to only a minor increase in the share of low sulphur fuel oil since, among other things, the low sulphur oil was still more expensive for customers than high sulphur fuel oil. It is worth noting in this case that the tax differential did not even reach a threshold level where regular and environmentally friendlier products would have the same price.[44] A threshold level is significant in other ways too, for instance, when an environmentally damaging product – like mercury batteries – is taxed to guide consumption towards a substitute benign product, such as to mercury-free batteries. A tax which keeps the price of the hazardous products below the price of benign products does not necessarily have very much effect.[45]

Technological and other constraints which surround the real-life choices have to be taken into account within this context, too. In relation to these constraints, we should note the conditions necessary to change over from leaded to unleaded petrol. First, there should be no technical restrictions; car engines must be able to run perfectly on the alternative fuel. Second, the environmentally more favourable fuel should be available as widely as possible in a relatively short period of time. A third issue worth noting is the use of cars with catalytic converters, and particularly the fact that these cars cannot run on leaded petrol without irreparable damage to the converter. Moreover, the international dimension in the introductory phase of unleaded petrol and catalyst converters should be taken into account. This dimension was important in Germany in the mid-1980s, when the national programme on catalytic converters was introduced. Cars were used for business and tourist trips abroad. Therefore, it was important that unleaded petrol was available not only in Germany but in other countries where trips were made.

Tax differentiations are also interesting from the perspective of dynamic efficiency. In the literature and sometimes in the preparatory drafts of legislation, environmental taxes have been legitimated by dynamic efficiency, that is they may encourage the search for and adoption of new environment-saving technology. However, it seems that technological development plays another role in the context of environmentally motivated tax differentiations. Technological development has paved the way for tax differentiations, meaning that these differentiations have been implemented only after new, environmentally friendly fuel qualities have been made.[46]

5.4.7 Basis of Incentive Environmental Taxes

The comprehensiveness of an incentive environmental tax obviously has a great impact on its environmental effectiveness. Many environmental taxes are narrow-based taxes, which restricts their possibilities of making significant improvements in the state of the environment; for instance, taxes on disposable items represent such taxes, if their effectiveness is evaluated in terms of the overall waste management policy. In this respect, general waste taxes may be superior to individual product taxes in reducing the volume of wastes.

For instance, a pesticide tax may offer a 'warning example' of the undesirable consequences of an incentive environmental tax, if its scope is limited and farmers are exempted from it.[47] This exemption may create conditions for tax fraud. Instead of buying in shops and paying the pesticide tax, people could buy pesticides through a local farmer and thus avoid the tax. More generally, tax evasion and inappropriate measures for avoiding tax may lead to serious difficulties concerning environmental effectiveness. For instance, if the tax rate is initially set at the target level x, but some of the polluters avoid the tax by inappropriate measures, the goal of the tax will not be reached. Therefore, the tax rate has to be increased, inducing inappropriate measures to an even larger extent than before. Since the goal will not be achieved, the tax rate has to be increased again, and so on. Consequently, there is a threat that inappropriate measures will lead to a 'vicious circle' in which tax increases follow each other without the environmental policy goal being achieved.

In general, 'pollutant recycling' is one inappropriate way of avoiding environmental taxes or other environmental regulation. For instance, strict regulation of water effluent may in the long run cause an increase in air effluent. Thus regulators should be cautious in their policy; it is not very helpful to concentrate on only one part of the environmental problems, and the regulatory approach should be comprehensive.

The choice of a proper legislative technique is also relevant here, and can be highlighted by an example from Finnish and Swedish fertilizer taxation. According to the previous Finnish Act on the Taxation of Phosphorous Fertilizers (§ 5(5)), 'fertilizers which are used as expendable raw material in the manufacturing of goods' were exempted from the tax. According to the fourth clause in the same paragraph 'fertilizers, which are used in the clean-up of waste waters based on biological clean-up' were also exempted from the tax. Thus, the legislative technique was to enumerate exhaustively the activities for which fertilizers were not taxed. In contrast, according to the Swedish Fertilizer Tax Act, a deduction from the tax can be made for such fertilizers 'which have been used or sold for purposes other than for usage as a plant nutrient'.

In practice, both legislative techniques can lead to a similar breadth in the fertilizer tax law. Technological progress, however, may lead to situations in which fertilizers will be used for completely new purposes, which do not cause a nutrient burden to waters as fertilizers used in plant cultivation do. The technique applied in Finnish legislation would mean that the fertilizers used for new purposes would be taxed only so long as the required amendments are not made to the legislation. In contrast, the Swedish legislative technique is externally flexible, because new usages of fertilizers do not require amendments in the law.

With respect to the environmental effectiveness of incentive environmental taxes, there is a connection between the comprehensiveness of the tax and the tax level. In other words, if the competitive products or activities are not included in the breadth of the tax, the possibilities of raising the tax rate would be limited. For instance, in the EU Member Countries the level of increase applied to heating fuels has been much lower than the level of increase of petrol and diesel oil taxes. One explanatory factor proposed for this phenomenon has been that certain directly competing products, for example, natural gas and coal, were outside the scope of the previous EU excise duty.

The linkage between environmental tax and the amount of pollution is crucial to environmental effectiveness.[48] For example, motor fuel tax will not reduce nitrogen oxide emissions, because it involves no incentive to choose motors with better cleaning technology. Therefore, an environmental differentiation of the motor vehicle tax or some other tax arrangements would be needed. Another example is offered by the carbon tax aimed at reducing carbon dioxide emissions implemented as *ad valorem* tax. Above all, there is no correlation between the transaction value of fossil fuels and carbon dioxide emissions. On the contrary, some of the cheaper fuels, such as coal, are associated with particularly high carbon dioxide emissions. Godard (1993) has even claimed that *ad valorem* taxes on fuels could potentially have the perverse effect of actually increasing carbon dioxide emissions. *Ad valorem* taxes might raise the prices of oil and natural gas relative to coal. Although such a tax would create an incentive to reduce total energy use, it would also create an incentive to increase the carbon intensity of the fuel mix. In contrast, the correlation between the quantities of fossil fuels burned and carbon dioxide emissions is a clear one, and therefore the carbon tax should be specific, expressed as a fixed amount per tonne of carbon.

In summary, in relation to the issue of linkage, a common view is that environmental tax should not be related to value, since normally the pollution associated with the production or use of a particular product is not a function of its value. In practice, the vast majority of environmental taxes comply with the linkage principle in the sense that the tax is connected to the carbon content of fossil fuels, the amount of nitrogen, phosphorous and cadmium in fertilizers, and/or the volume or weight of wastes. On the other hand, it has generally been thought that taxes based on measured emissions will be better linked to the amount of pollution than product-related environmental taxes. This view could gain in popularity if effluent taxes levied on all polluters were based on actually measured emissions. However, due to high measurement costs effluent taxes on minor pollution sources are often table-based taxes. Thus, the linkage between the amount of pollution and the amount of tax is weak in these circumstances. On the other hand, *ad quantum* taxes as such are not always appropriate instruments for reducing pollution, for example, from the cost-effectiveness point of view. An illustration of the relationship between environmental taxes and cost-effectiveness is offered by a motor fuel tax enacted to restrict nitrogen oxide emissions. One European study has calculated that this arrangement would cost 17 times more than a tax based on driving distance and the environmental characteristic of a motor vehicle.

Dynamic efficiency should not be omitted either. This consideration can be highlighted by a sulphur tax which is determined according to the value of the products. A tax of this kind may spur innovations which reduce the financial burden caused by the tax, but those innovations may be such that they do not promote the reduction of sulphur dioxide emissions into the environment in the best possible way. Moreover, *ad valorem* tax does not include any incentive to abate sulphur from emission exhausts and it would be very difficult to establish such a value-based sulphur tax which takes into account those emission reductions. On the contrary, a fuel tax based on sulphur content would easily permit the inclusion of an abatement system.[49]

The linkage principle (in addition to the transparency principle) is highly important from a legal point of view. First, the European Commission has taken this approach seriously in granting member states permission to apply for tax differentiations on fuel products. Approval has consistently required that the tax treatment is based on observable technical characteristics. Second, prohibiting the delegation of legislative power according to the legality principle should be taken into account here. It would be inconsistent if a covert delegation were allowed by the flexible tax norms, but at the same time the attitude to open delegation would be unresponsive.

5.4.8 Volatility/Stability of Incentive Environmental Taxes

The volatility of tax rates and structures substantially erodes the environmental effectiveness of environmental taxes. The Finnish carbon taxation can be cited as an extreme example. This tax was introduced in 1990 and the initial level was low. The tax rate doubled in 1993 and at the same time an electricity tax was introduced. At the beginning of 1994 the electricity tax was repealed and the energy tax was amended to include the carbon tax, and to tax fossil fuels used as inputs in generating electricity. In 1995 both the energy and carbon tax components were substantially increased. In the same year planning began for a new energy tax reform, which was implemented at the beginning of 1997. The electricity tax was reintroduced, fossil fuels used in generating electricity were exempted from the carbon tax and the energy tax component was eliminated. At the beginning of 1998 the scope of the electricity tax was altered and the carbon tax rate increased; finally, new energy tax relief was introduced in September 1998. In these circumstances it would almost be a miracle if the carbon tax were environmentally effective.[50]

One source of volatility in tax rates is the earmarking of tax proceeds from incentive environmental taxes. For instance, in addition to reducing nutrient pollution the purpose of the previous Finnish fertilizer tax was to finance the subsidies for surplus export production. Consequently, the fertilizer tax rate was determined by the revenue need in agricultural policy, thereby creating instability in fertilizer taxation because the revenue need varied annually. An important generalization can be made on the basis of this example. The proceeds from incentive environmental taxes should not be earmarked, because they easily create volatility in environmental tax legislation. This is partly due to the difficulty of determining which goal is preferable, the revenue need or the incentive purpose.

5.5 EFFICIENCY PROPERTIES OF INCENTIVE ENVIRONMENTAL TAXES

In short, there seems to be a gap between macro-policy and micro-policy levels in the role of cost-effectiveness.[51] When incentive environmental taxes are compared with direct regulation, cost-effectiveness is one of the main arguments supporting the introduction of a tax option as opposed to tightening direct regulation. However, at the micro-policy level, where the tax is designed, cost-effectiveness loses much of its position as a regulatory standard. When these taxes are analysed from micro-policy point of view, it appears that cost-effectiveness has been used – at least to some extent – as an illusory justification for incentive environmental taxes.

First, cost-effectiveness has become a major reason for legitimating incentive environmental taxes at the legislative level.[52] However, we cannot conclude that incentive environmental taxes, in effect, would approximate the least-cost means of reducing pollution, because so many compromises are made in these taxes at the micro-policy level. For instance, if the tax level is so low that an environmental tax does not influence the behaviour of polluters, such a tax can in no way be legitimated by cost-effectiveness. An extreme case occurs when the marginal tax rate is zero, as in table-based effluent taxes and ceiling provisions in carbon taxation.

Second, when direct regulation is a binding constraint in a mixed system, an environmental tax will have no effect on the level of pollution and, thus, does not improve the cost-effectiveness of environmental regulation.[53] In other words, if the tax does not guide the conduct of the polluters, it cannot do so cost-effectively.

Third, the variability of tax rates among polluters for non-environmental reasons also serves to weaken cost-effectiveness.[54] As we have seen, there are numerous tax relief procedures under carbon tax legislation, but this is only one example of the variability of the tax rates.

Fourth, narrow-based environmental taxes constitute distinct problems because they may be directed at activities which would be very expensive in reducing pollution.[55] On the other hand, it is problematic to broaden the scope of the tax to cover least-cost pollution sources because of the asymmetrical information between legislator and polluters.

Fifth, the linkage between pollution and the tax level is highly important. For instance, nitrogen oxide emissions are not directly related to the amount of petrol used and, thus, increasing petrol taxes would also be inappropriate for reducing these emissions from the cost-effectiveness point of view.

Sixth, shortcomings in technological flexibility are reflected as shortcomings in the cost-effectiveness of environmental taxes. Technological flexibility is clearly evident in the Swedish carbon tax: if the polluter manages to reduce carbon dioxide emissions while using fossil fuel, compensation proportionate to the reduction of emissions is granted. Incorporating an abatement system in carbon taxation would provide an incentive to develop technologies which eliminate carbon dioxide emissions from exhausts and is, therefore, also important from the dynamic efficiency point of view.

Finally, cost-effectiveness would be eroded by the unpredictability of tax treatment and tax legislation, as well as a too short timescale for the introduction of the tax.[56]

There are two differing approaches to the dynamic efficiency of incentive environmental taxes from the macro-policy point of view. The mainstream approach still states that environmental taxes provide a permanent incentive to reduce pollution and innovate even below target levels to reduce tax payments. The counterargument is that the burden of the tax leaves firms with fewer resources for R&D, and the creation of innovative, less-polluting methods of production may be slower than under direct regulation.

The empirical evidence concerning the dynamic efficiency of environmental taxes is only anecdotal. The Swedish charge on nitrogen oxide emissions is an example. The charge helped to significantly reduce emissions in the 1990s. Investments in new equipment, optimization of combustion, and the development of new control systems all contributed to the reduction of those emissions. More specifically, some plants sought to give employees an incentive to operate the process in the optimal manner by paying bonuses related to the demonstrated reduction in emissions. Selective non-catalytic reduction measures like the injection of urea or ammonia proved a cheap way of reducing emissions. Before the introduction of the charge such measures had not been used at all in Swedish plants. Another example concerns the German water effluent tax implemented in 1981. As a result, the clean water technology market has grown rapidly in Germany. According to some researchers, this development might also indicate that the water effluent tax has made some contribution to technical innovation. Moreover, Japan has been a world leader in technologies reducing sulphur dioxide emissions, and a sulphur tax has been in effect there since 1973.

Micro-policy considerations are worth noting within this context even though they may only lead to hypothetical conclusions. First, the speed at which environmental taxes are introduced can be critical in determining the response adopted by polluters. For instance, it has been suggested that too short a timescale will favour the adoption of end-of-pipe technologies since alternative clean technologies may not be immediately available. Second, an iterative, trial-and-error process is problematic because it will undermine the predictability of the tax treatment, and thereby also reduce the incentive for innovative activities. From this standpoint, a progressive timetable for setting the tax rates is a better alternative in environmental tax policy. Third, the structure of environmental tax rates may influence dynamic efficiency. For instance, the carbon tax rate on natural gas in Finland is only 50 per cent of what it would be if the tax rate were determined according to the carbon content of this fossil fuel. This tax relief is, of course, an incentive to increase the use of natural gas instead of coal and peat. On the other hand, the reduced tax rate on natural gas is a source of innovation bias. Because it is possible to produce energy with non-fossil fuels, the reduced tax rate on natural gas dilutes the incentives to move to non-fossil fuels. Fourth, the linkage between pollution and the tax level may be inappropriate, which distorts technological advances in the environmental field. For instance, a tax may be imposed on electricity even though the purpose of the tax is to spur the reduction of carbon dioxide emissions. The electricity tax, however, may not spur measures in the production of electricity which would limit the emitted emissions. Finally, the volatility of tax rates and structures essentially erodes both the environmental effectiveness and dynamic efficiency of environmental taxes.

NOTES

1   See OECD (1997) and OECD (1999). See Andersen (2003), 163 ff, on carbon tax in the Nordic countries.
2   See Helm and Pearce (1990), 2.
3   See OECD (1985), 189.
4   See Faure and Ubachs (2003), 27 ff.
5   See Mäler (1984), 444, and SOU 1990:59, 117.
6   De Clercq (1994), 51.
7   See Victor (1992), 247, and Godard (1993), 68.
8   See Huppes and Kagan (1989), 218–219.
9   Baumol and Oates (1988), 161.
10 See Rose-Ackerman (1973), 522–523, Anderson et al. (1977), 35, and Pezzey (1988), 221.
11 See OECD (1975), 97, and Oates (1994), 114.
12 See Barde (1997), 226.
13 See De Grauwe (1993), 34, and OECD (1993), 110.
14 SOU 1991:90, 12.
15 OECD (1988), 172.
16 See SOU 1994:114, 237.
17 See Jacobs (1991), 272, fn. 24.
18 See Zeckhauser (1981), 210.
19 Poterba (1993), 61–62.
20 See Bohm and Russell (1985), 438.
21 OECD (1993), 111.
22 See Hahn (1989), 49.
23 See Medhurst (1993), 45.
24 See OECD (1975), 71.
25 SOU 1990:59, 485.
26 See Surrey (1973), 168, and Anderson et al. (1977), 52–53.
27 See De Grauwe (1993), 34, and Smith (1997), 28.
28 See Surrey (1973), 168.
29 For these views, see Jaffe, et al. (1995), 132 ff, and Ekins (1996), 17–20.
30 See NOU 1992:3, 18.
31 See Stevens (1993), 8–9.
32 See OECD (2001), 77-78, and Majocchi and Missaglia (2003), 343 ff.
33 See Määttä (1997), 329 ff.
34 See SOU 1989:83, 273–274.
35 See Barker (1993), 251, and Smith and Vollebergh (1993), 220.
36 Rist and Eggler (1992), 63.
37 See Poterba (1991), 75, and TemaNord 1994: 561, 34–35.
38 Pearson and Smith (1991), 23, and Poterba (1991), 75.
39 See SOU 1991:90, 153–154.
40 Pearson and Smith (1991), 25.
41 See OECD (1997), 94.
42 See Gale and Barg (1995), 22, and Scnutenhaus (1995), 89.
43 See TemaNord 1996:568, 33.
44 Convery and Rooney (1996), 27–28.
45 Jacobs (1991), 143–144.
46 Määttä (1997), 153–154.
47 See De Clercq (1994), 59.

48 See Smith (1995), 21–23.
49 On abatement systems, see Määttä (1997), 296–299.
50 Määttä (1999), 323.
51 Määttä (1997), 149–154.
52 See SOU 1990:59, NOU 1992:3, and Km. 1993:35.
53 See Brown and Johnson (1984), 942.
54 See TemaNord 1994:561, 34–35.
55 See Ds. 1994:33, 67–68.
56 See Medhurst (1993), 45.

6. Financing Environmental Taxes

6.1 PRELIMINARY REMARKS

Financing environmental taxes are tax measures intended to raise revenue in pursuit of an environmental policy and an integral aspect of financing environmental taxes is that their proceeds are earmarked to that end. According to Wilkinson (1994), earmarking is understood here in the strong sense that the amount of revenue yielded by the tax determines the amount of spending. It also means that the rate of financing tax is determined by the amount of expenditure required for the programme.

The purpose of this chapter is to offer an overview of the main regulatory problems of financing environmental taxes. First, we analyse the regulatory problems related to the choice between incentive and financing environmental tax. In other words, which factors advocate the guidance of polluters' behaviour through tax incentives and which factors advocate the collection of revenue through taxation? Second, we examine the appropriateness of earmarking proceeds from environmental taxes. Third, we weigh the merits of financing environmental expenditures by financing environmental taxes or by proceeds from income and VAT. Thus, the overall purpose is to examine whether financing environmental taxes are appropriate tools in environmental policy.

Several types of financing environmental taxes are or have been in force in European countries. The following may be cited as examples:[1]

- A waste oil tax levied on lubricating oils intended to generate funds for collection and treatment of used waste oils.
- Financing aircraft noise charges/taxes usually levied in order to finance measures taken against noise pollution around airports.
- A tax refund system for car hulks consisting of two parts: first, funds for the system are collected usually as a surcharge on a motor vehicle tax; second, when the vehicle is delivered for scrap, a premium is paid.
- A tax refund system applied to the disposal of batteries. The tax may be based on the content of heavy metals in batteries. The battery tax, on the one hand, generates funds for the collection of used batteries

and, on the other han, may reduce the consumption of these articles.

- Financing waste taxes aimed at financing, for example, proper collection of waste. However, in many countries applying a waste tax, the tax is incentive in nature.
- An oil pollution tax in Finland levied on imported oil; one goal is to generate funds for the procurement of equipment for cleaning oil spills.

Some general remarks on financing environmental taxes are worth making. First, the total number of financing taxes is quite low compared with incentive taxes in western Europe. It is, however, somewhat misleading to claim that earmarking the proceeds from environmental taxes has been an important driving force in the emergence of an environmental tax policy.[2] This is emphasized by the fact that in the short history of environmental tax policy in western Europe many financing environmental taxes have already been repealed. Moreover, the proceeds from financing environmental taxes have usually been very small. Finally, in some cases it has been reported that financing environmental taxes, such as the Finnish waste oil tax and oil pollution tax, have fulfilled their task well.[3] In contrast, the Austrian waste tax has been criticized for not generating enough revenue, at least at the initial level.

Financing environmental taxes can be divided into three categories according to the purposes of earmarking tax proceeds. First, tax refund systems are otherwise similar to deposit refund systems except that the deposit is collected as a tax (or sometimes as a charge). Tax refund systems for car hulks and batteries constitute examples of this type of arrangement. Second, there are financing taxes of a reparative nature. The Finnish oil pollution tax is an example of one. The proceeds from the tax are mainly used for the equipment required in cleaning up oil spills. Waste tax may be designed to finance the clean-up of contaminated sites, for example, in Austria. Third, financing environmental taxes consists of taxes which are used to finance other public measures in environmental protection. For instance, aircraft noise taxes or charges are usually used to finance insulation measures employed around airports. Typically, the revenue from taxes on lubricant oils have been used to develop the infrastructure necessary for dealing with the proper collection, storage and disposal of used oil.

6.2   A FINANCING OR AN INCENTIVE ENVIRONMENTAL TAX?

In principle, all the environmental taxes which are currently incentive taxes can be redesigned as financing taxes. For instance, it has been suggested that a tax on beverage containers could be designed not to yield direct environmental benefits but to finance anti-litter campaigns.

Researchers are generally united in their recommendation that environmental taxes should be a means of inducing polluters to adopt less-polluting behaviour.[4] In other words, financing environmental taxes would not be appropriate tools in environmental policy. This would also mean that environmental taxes should always be set at a level which guarantees achieving the pollution reduction targets.

Even though the above-mentioned recommendation is compatible with the Pigouvian idea of environmental taxes, we cannot subscribe to it in all circumstances. First of all, it would work against promoting cost-effectiveness in environmental policy. Incentive environmental tax is, in principle, cost-effective if it is the cheapest way to reduce pollution at the source. However, the issue is not always so straightforward. For instance, it is possible that reducing damage by aircraft noise would be more expensive at the source, by moving to less noisy aircraft, than at the transmission stage of the noise or at the target of the noise problem. In such circumstances, a financing environmental tax which generates funds to provide for insulation measures around airports may be more cost-effective than an incentive environmental tax. The implementation of this regulatory option is by no means unproblematic.[5] In particular, asymmetrical information makes it difficult to make the recommendation operative satisfactorily: the legislator cannot be certain of which technical measures would be the cheapest in reducing the environmental problem. Therefore, it is not surprising that certain environmental taxes have been implemented in some countries as financing taxes and in other countries as incentive taxes.

Thus, Coase's (1960) critique of environmental taxes cannot be accepted. Coase claims that environmental taxes do not take into account the reciprocal nature of environmental problems. As noted, however, it is just a choice between an incentive and a financing tax, and this makes it possible to consider whether it is cheaper for the polluters or the victims of pollution (or a third party) to reduce pollution damage. Nevertheless, it should be admitted that asymmetrical information between regulators and regulatees makes it difficult to operationalize this regulatory option satisfactorily.

A second viewpoint is closely related to the waste oil tax, a tax which is usually levied on lubricants. The tax on lubricating oils should be very high in order to stimulate the use or development of more environmentally friendly alternatives. Therefore, we may claim that the more inelastic the demand for the taxable product, the more suitable it is for a financing tax. One reason is that the proceeds from such a tax would be stable. Another consideration is that environmental problems are not actually related to the use of lubricating oils, but to the disposal of waste oil. The overall conclusion is clear: a financing environmental tax on lubricating oils generating funds for a waste oil return system is a more appropriate instrument than an incentive environmental tax on these oils. In other words, a low financing environmental tax would be environmentally more effective in these circumstances than a high incentive one. More generally, incentive environmental taxes may be an appropriate way to deal with harmful products if they are levied on products such as fertilizers and pesticides, which cannot be recovered from the environment.[6] In contrast, if the improper disposal of waste rather than its generation *per se* is important, financing environmental taxes are more beneficial.[7]

There are also other reasons – mainly related to administrative issues – to sometimes opt for financing environmental taxes over incentive taxes.[8] With respect to waste tax, it has been observed that a financing waste tax could be levied at a lower rate than an incentive tax.[9] Thus, if there is a fear that a high incentive waste tax would result in illegal dumping, then an alternative would be to design the tax as financing in nature and thereby avoid or reduce inappropriate tax avoidance.[10] Moreover, an issue worth mentioning is the spatial nature of environmental problems. For instance, the use of pesticides causes problems, and their severity critically depends on the location. To be effective an incentive tax should be regionally differentiated, a practice which is, however, administratively very difficult to enforce. Thus, a regulatory option would be to enact a tax as a financing environmental tax which can be uniform across the country. In practice, pesticide taxes have been incentive in nature, even though they are levied uniformly across the country. It is worth noting the interdependence between the level of an environmental tax and the administrative problems it gives rise to. The higher the level of tax is, the more precisely the tax base has to be determined.[11] In other words, if it is impossible to precisely design an environmental tax, then a financing environmental tax may be a real option, since the rate of a financing tax is often lower than that of an incentive tax.

6.3 EARMARKING OF PROCEEDS FROM ENVIRONMENTAL TAXES

The discussion concerning earmarking proceeds from environmental taxes can be criticized on at least two grounds. First, no distinction has been made between different kinds of environmental taxes; the appropriateness of earmarking has simply been evaluated as if it affected all environmental taxes in a similar way.[12] Moreover, it seems that no distinction has been made between environmental taxes and other taxes in respect of this issue. The conventional view of public economics states that earmarking is an inefficient arrangement.[13]

Second, and related to the above, the argumentation has been defective. In many papers, the need for earmarking is justified by acceptability alone:[14] earmarking creates public acceptance and political support for new environmental taxes. In this sense, earmarking is a legitimacy strategy; it is often necessary in real life even though it may lead to inappropriate regulation. The literature also refers to fiscal transparency:[15] earmarking indicates to the public and the polluters that proceeds are used in a legitimate way.

Earmarking has been criticized on the basis of general tax policy arguments in relation to the power of the legislator on budget issues being reduced in scope. This would, in turn, lead to inefficient public spending because the legislator cannot allocate the proceeds to targets in which the social marginal benefit would be greatest.[16] In addition, the OECD (1996) has warned about a 'precedent effect': if the proceeds from environmental taxes are earmarked, demands to earmark funds from other taxes could be made concerning other objectives.

The tax policy standpoint mentioned above is biased since, among other things, it ignores the idea that there are several ways to implement an earmarking policy. Nevertheless, the argument may hold, particularly when a so-called fund procedure is applied: proceeds from a tax are channelled into a separate fund, which can decide independently on how the tax proceeds will be used. The situation changes in a budget procedure: the proceeds from a tax are channelled towards the budget. This means that the legislator can decide on the tax design and rates as well as the use of the proceeds from the tax. It is difficult to claim here that the budget power of the legislator would be eroded.

The issues surrounding the earmarking of environmental tax proceeds make up an extensive topic, one that is not only related to matters of acceptability and pure tax policy. For instance, Barde and Owens (1993) claim that 'earmarking may increase the reliability of funds for environment programmes, which is important when the public sector is operating under tight fiscal constraints'. Even though this argument may hold in certain circumstances, it is not always valid. First, very much depends on the fiscal stability of an earmarked tax. For instance, if the tax is directed at a product which is prone to very elastic demand, such taxation will lead to a financial crisis in the system. More generally, an important challenge within this context is to find ways of stabilizing the proceeds from financing taxes.

Second, the above argument overlooks the possibility that public agencies may act strategically.[17] It has long been acknowledged that these agencies promote their own interests as well. Moreover, von Weitzäcker and Jesinghaus (1992) maintain that the earmarking of tax proceeds may mean an expanded role for government and thereby an increase in bureaucracy. In addition, the earmarking of taxes for specific purposes may inhibit any offsetting reductions in distortionary taxes, such as income taxes. On the other hand, problems are alleviated by the fact that financing environmental taxes have been fiscally insignificant in practice.

Distinct from financing environmental taxes, the proceeds from incentive environmental taxes should not be earmarked.[18] If an environmental tax affects the behaviour of polluters in a desired way, there is simply no need to earmark the proceeds. In addition, the Tinbergen rule is again worth noting: it is difficult to realize two objectives with a single instrument other than by chance. With regard to incentive environmental taxes, this means that either the incentive impact of the tax or the financing goal will suffer if the proceeds are earmarked.[19]

6.4 FINANCING ENVIRONMENTAL TAXES OR FUNDS FROM GENERAL TAX PROCEEDS?

As mentioned above, the goal of financing environmental taxes is to generate funds for environmental protection. Furthermore, the regulatory option of financing environmental taxes is to generate funds for environmental protection from general tax revenues.[20]

Attitudes towards product-related financing taxes indicate that the higher the sales of taxable products are, the higher the revenues are from the taxes and the better they serve their goal.[21] However, the trade-off is not necessarily so paradoxical. If there is a close linkage between the amount of taxable products and the expenditures for environmental protection, taxing these objects may reduce the revenue need. It is the revenue need, not the actual amount of revenues as such, which is critical. For instance, the costs of waste oil management arise mainly from the use of lubricating oils. Therefore, a tax on lubricating oils reduces the need for expenditures in waste oil management if the tax reduces the use of these oils. In a similar fashion, the financing tax on batteries, which would reduce the sale of these items, diminishes the revenue need for their collection and disposal. No such gain exists when environmental protection measures are financed through general tax receipts.

The relative merit of financing environmental taxes compared with general tax proceeds is also that regulatory provisions may be incorporated into the financing taxes. For instance, the oil pollution tax in Finland has been differentiated on the basis of the environmental safety of cargo ships.[22] Lubricating oils, which are made of waste oil, are exempted from the Finnish tax on this oil. This exemption is justified by the promotion of the reuse of waste oil and thereby also promotes waste oil management. Moreover, it is worth mentioning that the Dutch water effluent tax has spurred the reduction of waste water, even though it was initially a financing tax.

In summary, if the financing environmental tax can be implemented so that the tax reduces the revenue need for environmental protection measures, it may provide a more appropriate source of revenue than general tax proceeds. These examples of how regulatory provisions are incorporated into financing environmental taxes further illustrate that in practice there is no sharp distinction between financing and incentive taxes.

If the expenditures funded by a financing environmental tax are stable year after year, the proceeds from the tax should also be stable. For instance, the motor fuel tax may be superior to the motor vehicle tax as a source of revenue financing the refund system for car hulks. The reason is simply the fact that the proceeds from motor fuel taxes are quite stable with respect to cycles of recession and boom whereas the proceeds from motor vehicle tax react sensitively to those fluctuations. Consequently, the more unstable the revenue source for the potential financing tax is, the greater the justification is to collect funds by conventional taxes.

Furthermore, one may also claim that financing environmental taxes are more compatible with the polluter-pays principle than the use of general tax receipts to cover the costs of some specific environmental measures. In other words, financing environmental taxes shift the burden of financing environmental protection measures from the taxpayers to the polluters. For instance, the introduction of the Finnish tax on waste oil was justified by the fact that the largest part of the waste oil problem is generated from lubricating oils and therefore the tax was specifically directed at these items. In addition, financing charges on aircraft noise have been regarded as largely compatible with the polluter-pays principle.

A problem related to narrow-based taxes, such as financing environmental taxes, is that they are vulnerable to international tax competition and to cross-border shopping. When expenditures are financed by broad-based taxes, even very low increases in the tax rates may be enough, but with narrow-based taxes the tax rates have to be high in order to cover expenditures. For instance, tax refund systems on batteries may be vulnerable to cross-border shopping in two respects. First, if a battery tax is set too high, it will encourage people to buy batteries abroad. Second, high refund rates encourage people to return both taxed and untaxed batteries. Consequently, there would be minor proceeds from a financing tax but high expenditures because of the refund payments. If the tax refund system is corrected by an increase in the tax rates, the situation even worsens. In such circumstances, it would be more appropriate to cover the costs of environmental protection measures through general tax receipts than by financing environmental taxes.

Finally, administrative limitations are critically important when considering alternatives for financing environmental policy measures. For instance, one of the strengths of the tax refund system for car hulks in Sweden was its administrative simplicity.[23] The administrative costs are moderate in this case, because the tax refund system can be implemented as part of existing motor vehicle taxation. The situation may change drastically, for instance, if the excise tax system cannot be utilized, but the financing tax is implemented as an effluent tax.

NOTES

1 See Määttä (1997), 58–62.
2 Cf. Smith (1992), 39, and Barde and Owens (1996), 13.
3 Km. 1993:35, 27.
4 See Barde and Opschoor (1994), 24–25, and Barde and Owens (1996), 14.
5 See TemaNord 1994:561, 92.
6 Opschoor and Vos (1989), 115.
7 Stavins and Whitehead (1992), 29.
8 See OECD (1989), 159.
9 SOU 1990:59, 587.
10 See Copeland (1991), 144.
11 See Opschoor and Vos (1989), 114.
12 See OECD (1993), 102.
13 On attitudes towards earmarking among economists, see Wilkinson (1994), 122.
14 See Smith (1992), 38–39, Andersen (1994), 210, Paulus (1995), 65, and Barde and Owens (1996), 13.
15 See Barde and Opschoor (1994), 25.
16 See Musgrave and Musgrave (1989), 222.
17 See Surrey (1973), 168–169, and von Weitzäcker and Jesinghaus (1992), 17.
18 OECD (1991), 12.
19 See Smith (1992), 38.
20 See OECD (1993), 68–69.
21 Opschoor and Vos (1989), 115.
22 See TemaNord 1994:561, 58.
23 OECD (1980), 82–83.

7. Environmental Taxes from the Fiscal Point of View

7.1 PRELIMINARY REMARKS

Measuring the revenues of environmental taxes is not without problems. First, one reason is that the scope of environmental taxes is ambiguous. Using a narrow definition of environmental taxes, which only includes incentive environmental taxes, revenues prove to be much smaller than when using a broad definition of environmental taxes, which takes into account all the different types of environmental tax.[1]

Second, when an environmental tax is imposed as part of some existing tax, it may be difficult to determine exactly the revenues produced by the incentive environmental tax component. This problem has concerned the carbon tax in Finland, which was implemented on top of the existing fuel taxes. The problem emerges because the official balances of accounts do not separate revenue figures for the carbon tax, but include the revenue from the entire fuel tax.

Third, how can the revenues from environmental differentiation of fuel and vehicle taxes and redistributive taxes be determined? Here the view is that these taxes represent non-revenue-generating taxes. On the other hand, tax differentiations, like catalytic converter discounts, are not included in tax expenditures within the calculations of tax proceeds. Nevertheless, some fiscal confusion has arisen in evaluating this feature. For instance, France and Ireland have regarded the lower tax rate on unleaded petrol as a tax expenditure which constitutes a loss of tax proceeds compared with the normative petrol tax.[2] In contrast, the tax differentiation favouring unleaded petrol has been seen in Norway as a revenue-generating surcharge on leaded petrol.[3] In any case, a common trend in OECD countries has been that tax differentiation is classified neither as a revenue-generating tax nor as a tax expenditure. Moreover, the proceeds from environmental taxes are usually presented as gross figures. On the one hand, they may overstate the contribution of environmental taxes to national revenues, because environmental taxes are, under certain conditions, deductible in corporate income taxation. On the other hand, gross figures may understate this contribution, since these taxes are incorporated into the tax base of the VAT, again under certain conditions. In addition, the amount of transfer payments, connected to the consumer price index, may change due to the introduction or the raising of environmental taxes.

Of course, administrative costs should be taken into account when net receipts from environmental taxes are examined. Administrative costs have chiefly been minimized, in practice, by two factors. First, systems for identifying product characteristics have often been established by direct regulation prior to the introduction of environmental taxes.[4] Second, the introduction of environmental taxes has often meant that the tax bases of the existing excise taxes have been amended to some degree, or in some cases excise taxation has offered procedures for levying environmental taxes.[5] What is of great importance here is that environmental taxes have usually been implemented as product taxes, not as effluent taxes.

The receipts from environmental taxes vary significantly. The primary way of differentiating between environmental taxes is to distinguish between non-revenue-generating and revenue-generating environmental taxes. Revenue-generating environmental taxes have been classified into three groups.[6] In the case of very small environmental taxes the tax receipts are under 0.1 per cent of the total tax receipts, usually very clearly under 0.1 per cent. Financing environmental taxes are usually included in this group. In addition, several incentive environmental taxes can be classified as very small taxes, for instance, taxes on disposable cameras and razors, the tax on disposable tableware and the tax on pesticides. Swedish fertilizer tax and sulphur tax also belong to this group.

Small environmental taxes are such taxes where the proceeds are over 0.1 per cent but under 1.0 per cent of the total tax receipts. Examples of this class are the vehicle tax based on fuel consumption in Austria, the Danish, Dutch, Finnish and UK waste tax, Danish water tax and the previous fertilizer tax in Finland. Among incentive environmental taxes, the carbon tax is currently the one and only medium environmental tax, meaning the tax receipts from it are at least 1 per cent of the total tax receipts. The main source of the tax proceeds from fiscal environmental taxes has been the petrol tax. On the other hand, petrol tax shares vary significantly between countries. The level of diesel fuel tax is usually lower than the level of petrol tax. This is, of course, reflected in the proceeds from this tax, but in any case, diesel fuel oil tax may often be classified as a medium tax. The environmental tax mix varies greatly from country to country. For instance, Denmark and Greece heavily tax motor vehicles compared to the taxation on fuels, whereas the inverse is more common in many other parts of the western Europe. On the other hand, taxes on mineral oils are a main element of energy taxation in every country in western Europe.

A large share of incentive and financing environmental taxes applied in practice are either non-revenue-generating or very small environmental taxes. From this point of view environmental taxation has been a part of environmental policy rather than fiscal policy. It means, for instance, that the appropriateness of many environmental taxes has to be evaluated solely on environmental considerations.[7] The double-dividend gain which is often connected to environmental taxes is not important.[8] This means that the basis for revenue recycling is very limited. In other words, it is not possible to finance, for instance, income tax reductions with such environmental taxes that generate no or only extremely small amounts of revenue. On the other hand, the impact of such taxes on income distribution is minor. Furthermore, the disadvantage often connected to environmental taxes, that they are regressive, is of no importance. Sometimes environmental taxes have been criticized because their introduction would have inflationary consequences.[9] This statement is also irrelevant with respect to the bulk of environmental taxes.

Finally, it should be noted that the above-mentioned categorization of environmental taxes is not unambiguous, because it has only been made in respect of existing tax proceeds. The potential proceeds may be of interest when tax reforms are planned. They may be rather different from the proceeds and tax shares which have been presented here. However, empirical studies concretize one self-evident matter: it is impossible to generate large revenue from a tax which is fiscally very narrow-based.[10]

Another consideration arises from the changes in the long-term behaviour of polluters. Currently, the proceeds of some environmental taxes may still be rather high but when the polluters change their production processes and consumers their consumption patterns, the proceeds of a tax may be exhausted. Breakthroughs in technological innovations may lead to startling drops in the proceeds from an environmental tax.

7.2 ALTERNATIVE WAYS OF USING TAX PROCEEDS

Three possible ways can be distinguished to use the tax proceeds generated by environmental taxes. First, environmental taxes may be used to finance public expenditures, generally in the same way as taxes are usually applied. Second, tax proceeds can be earmarked for environmental protection or other purposes. Third, tax proceeds can be refunded to taxpayers.

When environmental taxes are examined as a traditional source of revenue, an important question is how to use the proceeds: whether to raise the total tax rate or to reduce other taxes by the amount generated by environmental taxes. In every country in which environmental tax policy has been discussed to a larger extent, the latter alternative has been emphasized. Revenue neutrality and revenue recycling have been key words in the policy discussion.

A distinction can be made between general and selective revenue recycling. General revenue recycling implies the introduction of environmental taxes or increasing their levels without affecting total revenues, and without targeting the reduction of other taxes to the target groups of environmental taxes. For instance, income tax reductions or reductions in the VAT rate may be financed by the proceeds from environmental taxes. In the case of selective revenue recycling, the introduction of environmental taxes or the raising of tax levels is done without changing the amount of revenue collected from a certain group of taxpayers, in this case those who are subject to the environmental tax. Selective revenue recycling can be implemented in two ways. First, it can reflect a change in a tax base, especially under energy taxation. Second, selective revenue recycling may be implemented by reducing other taxes on the target group.[11]

When environmental taxes are introduced on an individual basis, there are usually only narrow possibilities for general revenue recycling, because the proceeds of individual taxes are small. There is, however, a possibility for selective revenue recycling. When there is a desire for general revenue recycling, some kind of 'reform package' is usually necessary; for example, a large number of environmental taxes to facilitate the financing of income tax reduction.[12]

Identifying a case of earmarking is sometimes difficult because the expenditures of some environmental policy sector may be increased at the same time as an environmental tax is introduced into this sector. This has sometimes been the case with waste taxes. There is no formal earmarking of tax proceeds but the expenditures in waste management policy have been increased due to the introduction of the tax or an increase in the tax rate.[13] Earmarking tax proceeds can occur either by using a fund method or a budget method. In the fund method the proceeds generated by a tax are paid into a fund outside the budget. In the budget method the proceeds are channelled into the budget. The earmarking of tax proceeds differs from case to case according to the length of period in which the proceeds and expenditures are balanced.

Earmarking tax proceeds should not be confused with redistributive taxes.[14] These taxes are classified here as incentive environmental taxes. Redistributive taxes can be classified into two groups according to the basis of the refund system. First, in design-based refund systems tax proceeds are returned to polluters in the form of subsidies for new pollution control equipment. Another redistributive tax system is called a performance-based refund system. The factor distinguishing it from the design-based refund systems is that in redistribution the performance-based system is not connected to some specified investments made by the polluters.

7.3 SUITABILITY OF ENVIRONMENTAL TAXES FROM THE FISCAL POINT OF VIEW

7.3.1 Buoyancy of Tax Proceeds

Buoyancy of tax proceeds reflects the effect on tax proceeds when all changes in legislation and taxpayers' behaviour are taken into account. Since the aim of reducing pollution is inherent in most incentive environmental taxes, the buoyancy of tax proceeds may in the long run be below unity. This is a clear disadvantage from the fiscal standpoint. However, stability varies greatly. For instance, the carbon tax may provide a sustainable tax base from the fiscal point of view as long as economically viable means for reducing carbon dioxide emissions from exhausts are not developed. On the other hand, the technological development in the field of water effluent purification has in recent years led to the erosion of the tax base of water effluent taxes.

Particularly in the case of fiscal environmental taxes, the conflicting aims involved cannot easily be dismissed. For example, balance-of-payments factors, employment considerations, distributional consequences, safety of traffic, in addition to fiscal and environmental objectives are all factors that compound the difficulties of 'stabilizing' taxation. On the other hand, environmental taxes differ with respect to their vulnerability to these pitfalls.

What should we do if after a certain time the guidance effect becomes so strong that revenue begins to shrink? It has been suggested that new environmental taxes should be introduced.[15] This recommendation is problematic because it connects the use of environmental taxes to their future revenue yield. If tax proceeds diminish, new objects for environmental taxes would have to be found to compensate for the reduction in tax proceeds. The threat is that environmental taxes would be directed at activities where there is no need for taxation from the environmental standpoint. On the other hand, unless the tax proceeds diminish, would there be any reason for enlarging the scope of environmental taxation, even though there are environmental reasons for it? Of course, new environmental taxes may compensate for the revenue shortfall of existing environmental taxes to the extent that there are sound environmental policy reasons for introducing them.

Another option for offsetting the revenue shortfall is if the government again resorts to more conventional taxes.[16] However, this may be difficult for political reasons. Consequently, this policy option involves a threat to future budget deficits. Finally, a progressive time schedule may be applied in setting environmental tax rates.[17] This will stabilize the tax proceeds if polluters reduce pollution at the same time as the tax rate increases. There are many other reasons which favour this strategy, even though the strategy is not without defects. Therefore, the decision to apply a progressive implementation should be made after taking all these advantages and disadvantages into account, and not just on the basis of revenue stability.

7.3.2 Elasticity of Tax Proceeds

One aspect of revenue stability is the elasticity of environmental tax proceeds. This reflects what would happen to revenue receipts in the absence of amendments to legislation and changes in taxpayers' behaviour, or how environmental taxes and their receipts adjust to inflationary circumstances. For instance, VAT has an elasticity of unity, since it is an *ad valorem* tax, which offers an automatic hedge against inflation. The elasticity of all kinds of environmental tax proceeds is usually below unity, since these taxes are often *ad quantum* taxes, and their real value decreases with inflation. In this respect, the revenue stability in real terms of almost all environmental taxes is weaker than the stability of the proceeds from VAT. There are two exceptions to this: on the one hand, there are some *ad valorem* environmental taxes, and on the other hand, indexation may be applied in respect of environmental taxes.

Let us analyse the adjustment of incentive environmental tax rate to inflation in more detail. Inflation would result in lower emissions' control, because the real rate of an incentive tax declines with inflation if the nominal tax rate remains the same, unless a tax is an *ad valorem* tax. In this sense, *ad quantum* or specific environmental taxes are generally externally inflexible. For instance, an annual inflation rate of 5 per cent means that the real tax rate will decrease by about 30 per cent in five years. This would weaken the environmental effectiveness of a tax and also diminish the real share of proceeds from the environmental taxes.[18] In any case, one advantage of an *ad valorem* tax compared with an *ad quantum* tax is that it offers an automatic hedge against inflation. There is no need to raise the nominal tax rate, because the real tax rate also remains unchanged under inflationary conditions. However, there are severe drawbacks with an *ad valorem* environmental tax. In general, the linkage between pollution and the tax is better when the tax is related to quantities rather than values, since normally pollution is a function of the amount of the physical characteristics of a commodity rather than its value.[19] Therefore, a specific tax is a better instrument for internalizing external costs and can be better attuned to the level of external costs or in accomplishing the desired environmental policy goals.[20]

Ad valorem rates are also problematic with respect to cost-effectiveness and dynamic efficiency criteria. Because an *ad valorem* tax would wipe out the substitution effects, a given environmental objective can only be attained at higher costs. This is also reflected by the fact that *ad valorem* taxes would need a higher tax rate than one determined according to the linkage principle in order to achieve the same environmental policy target. A further disadvantage of an *ad valorem* tax is that it would not promote the best possible development and diffusion of environmentally beneficial technology. One further argument against *ad valorem* taxation is that these rates would apply not only to the products themselves, but also to the costs of advertising, packaging, and so on, all of which constitute the price of the product. Thus, *ad valorem* taxation arbitrarily increases the price differential in relation to other products.[21] For instance, *ad valorem* rates levied on fuel prices tend to tax distribution and marketing costs, something that is clearly unwarranted.[22] On the other hand, an *ad quantum* tax only taxes items which generate external costs and whose value, therefore, should not be included in the tax base. This feature of *ad valorem* taxation may also create incentives for inappropriate tax avoidance, because the taxpayers can easily 'manipulate' the amount of their tax. Furthermore, undesirable practices can be countered by levying the tax as early as possible in the production–distribution chain, and it is most appropriate to do this by levying an *ad quantum* tax. This is due to the fact that if collected at the manufacturing stage, *ad quantum* taxes do not require information about the ultimate retail price.[23]

Inflationary corrections mean that the rates of specific taxes are increased from time to time under inflationary conditions to preserve their real value. For instance, an OECD report (1996) has recommended that the specific rate be re-examined periodically, and if necessary readjusted to reflect changes in external circumstances. Another possibility would be to index tax rates to some price level measurement, for example, the consumer price index. This type of regulation has been recommended extensively. Indexation was introduced in Sweden in 1995 for energy and carbon taxes. In other words, a shift from nominal to real taxation has taken place in Sweden with respect to these taxes.

Both regulatory options have their pros and cons. One disadvantage of the correction procedure is that an increase in the tax rate may be politically unpopular, although it only serves to preserve the real value of the tax. A further consideration militating against the correction procedure and favouring indexation is that in several cases inflationary corrections in *ad quantum* taxes have in practice not been made for a long period. It also seems that interest in making corrections to tax rates depends on economic circumstances. In particular, when the economy is in recession, tax rate corrections have been rare.

The indexation procedure also has its disadvantages. First, in those cases where automatic indexation of excise rates has been applied, difficulties have arisen. For instance, in Canada and Denmark such an arrangement was applied and quickly abandoned. This was because indexation entails a number of technical problems in achieving the correct index given time lags. Second, indexation may limit the scope of decision-making if the government wishes, for other reasons, to vary the tax rate.[24] In particular, amendments in the rates of environmental taxes may be needed because of more stringent environmental policy goals or because the original tax rate was too low to achieve the desired goals. Inflationary corrections can be made within the context of these re-evaluations. In addition, if a progressive implementation is used in setting incentive tax rates, the necessary inflationary corrections can be made through increased tax rates.

7.3.3 Fiscal Flexibility

One consideration for evaluating taxes from the fiscal point of view is the ease of raising the tax rate to generate additional revenue; in other words fiscal flexibility can be discussed in this context.[25] For instance, one advantage in VAT is the relative ease of raising the VAT rate if additional revenue is needed.[26] The situation is the reverse with environmental taxes.

Because environmental taxes are fiscally narrow-based taxes, very significant increases in the tax rate are required compared with an increase in the VAT rates or income tax. In addition, depending on the tax object, the increase in the tax rate may lead to a reduction in tax proceeds, if pollution diminishes more than the increase in the tax rate. Moreover, very high tax rates will make environmental taxes vulnerable to international tax competition. In other words, cross-border shopping may increase substantially and the relocation effect may become a reality. Another essential point of view here is that the increase in the rate of an environmental tax based solely on an additional revenue need may conflict with respect to environmental policy considerations. Furthermore, the predictability of tax treatment argues for stability in environmental taxes, not their use as a means of generating additional revenue each year at varying tax rates. The predictability of tax treatment is a cornerstone for the environmental effectiveness and efficiency properties of environmental taxes.

7.3.4 Fiscal Illusion

The notion of fiscal illusion is associated with the misperception of the tax burden, that is of the amount of tax paid. It usually refers to a positive version of fiscal illusion meaning that the taxpayers regard their tax burden as smaller than it actually is. In fact, it is true that there are many potential sources of fiscal illusion under environmental taxation.[27]

First, environmental taxes are fragmented over a large group of taxes.[28] On the other hand, this state of affairs may be justified by the nature of the environmental problems regulated. Second, the implementation of environmental taxes mainly as product-related environmental taxes has meant that environmental taxes have at the same time been incorporated into the price of these products.[29] However, this feature of environmental tax policy is quite easy to explain since, due to practical reasons, effluent taxes may in general be limited to stationary sources of pollution. On the other hand, the polluting inputs, like nitrogenous fertilizers, can be taxed at moderate administrative costs. Third, it has been possible to levy environmental taxes in an established and thereby convenient way by 'piggy-backing' these taxes onto existing excise taxation procedures. Fourth, manipulation of the language has been common.[30] The use of the 'charge' instead of 'tax' is one expression of this and another is the enlargement of the scope of environmental taxes to cover some taxes which are primarily fiscally motivated. Finally, it appears that the public's attitude to environmental taxes is pervasive, which is shown by some poll data. In spite of these features, we should not ignore the fact that the largest part of environmental taxes is of such minor fiscal significance that the fiscal illusion is, in effect, only of theoretical interest.

A related point of view is the phenomenon generally called 'revenue addiction'. For instance, Barde and Owens (1996) have expressed concern by stating that 'although environment authorities will try to apply a rate high enough to achieve the environmental goal of the tax, treasuries may prefer to opt for a lower tax, which is less environmentally effective but ensures a more sustainable and predictable revenue yield'.

Within the context of revenue addiction, the sole consideration has been the manipulation of the tax level, or setting too low a level to affect the behaviour of polluters. However, another way of 'implementing' revenue addiction is to manipulate the tax base in such a way that limits the possibilities of reducing the tax burden. For instance, the carbon tax on fossil fuels used in electricity production may be replaced by a general tax on electricity. Consequently, the only way to avoid the tax is to reduce the consumption of electricity. Unlike a tax based on the carbon content of fossil fuels, there is no possibility of reducing the tax burden by moving to non-fossil fuels or to low-carbon fossil fuels. A mixed system is also a way to stabilize the proceeds from environmental taxes. Under conditions in which direct regulation is a binding constraint for polluters, environmental tax is *de facto* a fiscal tax. In other words, only direct regulation, not environmental tax, can guide the conduct of polluters.

Double-dividend gain or double-dividend illusion? Double-dividend gain means that environmental taxes may correct a market failure in the economy while at the same generating public revenues; these revenues in turn facilitate the reduction of those taxes which generate an excess burden in the economy.[31] But is double-dividend more fiction than fact?[32] First, double-dividend gain is not important in many environmental taxes, because they generate none or only extremely small amounts of revenue; this was demonstrated earlier. Second, an integral part of the hypothesis is that such taxes are reduced which generate an excess burden on the economy. However, in practice environmental taxes may, in effect, be needed for financing the reduction of other excise duties, in particular tobacco and alcohol taxes. An issue worth noting here is that tobacco and alcohol taxes are aimed at internalizing external costs (as well as environmental taxes). In this respect, financing the declining proceeds from tobacco and alcohol taxes by environmental taxes does not create, even theoretically, a basis for double-dividend gain. Third, it is indisputable that revenue neutrality has been critical in legitimating increases and rearrangements of environmental taxes. It is, however, questionable whether the increases in the rates of environmental taxes have actually been revenue-neutral. One example is the Finnish total tax ratio, which increased during 1990s, and at the same time the proceeds from environmental taxes increased.

Finally, double-dividend gain is questionable from the environmental perspective. The integral part of the hypothesis states that environmental taxes reduce pollution or the use of natural resources. However, empirical evidence does not clearly indicate that these taxes have always been environmentally effective. Numerous reasons may explain this phenomenon. For instance, marginal tax rates have been too low; environmental taxes have not comprehensively covered pollution sources; the linkage between the amount of pollution and environmental tax has not been appropriate; and the volatility of environmental tax legislation has essentially eroded the environmental effectiveness of these taxes.

We have discussed the positive version of fiscal illusion and an example is now necessary to illustrate the negative version. Because environmental taxes are usually *ad quantum* or specific taxes not related to the value of the product, the real rate of environmental taxes declines with inflation. One way to react is to apply inflationary corrections and increase the rates of specific taxes from time to time under inflationary conditions to preserve their real value. One disadvantage of inflationary corrections is that the increase in the tax rates may be politically unpopular, although it is only a question of preserving the real value of the tax. Thus, the resistance can be seen as an expression of a negative version of fiscal illusion.[33]

7.3.5 Distributional Consequences

In rem taxes, taxes on 'things', are imposed on activities or objects as such, independently of the characteristics of the taxpayer and in contrast to personal taxes, which are adjusted to the taxpayer's personal ability to pay. *In rem* taxes may be imposed on either the household or the firm. Personal taxes must be imposed on the household side of the transaction, since this offers a means of taking into account the taxpayer's personal ability to pay.[34]

Environmental taxes can be classified as *in rem* taxes, since they are taxes on products, effluents, wastes and other 'things'. Therefore, the ability to pay is not relevant to the design of environmental taxes. First, it is possible that the polluting firm will have to pay annual environmental taxes, which will effectively eliminate all its profits and may lead to its bankruptcy. Second, this property may also cause problems with income distribution, regressive impacts, and may require corrective measures. Third, it also means that the opportunities to use, for example, energy and motor vehicle taxes as social policy tools would be limited. In other words, environmental taxes should be levied irrespective of the polluter and the nature of the activity. On the other hand, regulatory taxes, like incentive environmental taxes, cannot be justified solely on the basis that target groups have had high profits.

The *in rem* and the regulatory natures of incentive environmental taxes suggest that public agencies too should be subject to the tax. This is important, since in practice public agencies have proven difficult to regulate, that is environmental authorities have had more success in curtailing emissions from private sources than those from government facilities. The *in rem* nature of environmental taxes may create difficult legitimacy problems. This problem can be highlighted by the experience of the property tax, which is also an *in rem* tax.[35] Taxpayers frequently regard the tax as unfair because the amount of property tax paid is (in many countries) decided with little or no regard to the personal circumstances of the taxpayer. In other words, the link between property tax paid and income is considered weak. It can be claimed that the link between environmental tax and income or profits of the polluters is even weaker than with property tax. Such consideration may, for instance, lead to the assumption that environmental taxes are not as acceptable in the business sector as corporate income tax is, because the latter tax is levied only if there are profits.

In principle, it is feasible to take account of ability to pay in environmental tax policy by means of three methods.[36] First, it is possible to apply general or selective revenue recycling. With respect to general revenue recycling, a poor candidate would be the reduction of progressive income tax rates, because it may lead to a double-regressive impact rather than to mitigate the regressive impacts of environmental taxes. The reduction of proportional income taxes avoids this effect, but it suffers from a displacement effect: those who do not pay income tax, such as students and pensioners, do not benefit from this revenue-recycling option. The VAT rate could be lowered to counterbalance the regressive impact of environmental taxes and avoid these undesirable effects.[37] However, selective revenue recycling may be a better alternative since it can be directed at those agents who suffer most from the regressive impact of an environmental tax. On the other hand, EU law significantly restricts opportunities to reduce the VAT rates of many single commodity groups.

The second option is to include distributional considerations in the design of the tax. For instance, the so-called threshold tax has been recommended in this context. It is also possible to discuss the target load principle here. For instance, with respect to the fertilizer tax, a threshold tax would mean that tax is imposed only on purchases of fertilizers which exceed a basic quantity per hectare. This tax-free allowance has been applied in the Dutch regulatory energy tax.[38] It goes without saying that threshold taxes are often administratively burdensome and sluggish. Moreover, other properties of a good environmental tax, such as cost-effectiveness, may be eroded due to the threshold tax.

A third option for mitigating regressive impacts is to make direct grants to those who suffer most from these impacts. This means, however, that the margin for revenue recycling is substantially narrowed, which may have a bearing on the acceptability of the tax. The increase in public expenditure through environmental taxes would also mean that the potential double-dividend gain is lost. Actual calculations have shown that if environmental tax proceeds are not offset by a reduction in other (distorting) taxes, economic growth would decline and unemployment increase.

On the other hand, most incentive and financing environmental taxes are so minor from the fiscal point of view that their distributional consequences can be ignored. In addition, the distributional impacts of energy-related taxes are not necessarily regressive and mitigation measures are unnecessary. Finally, distributional impacts of environmental taxes should not be viewed in isolation but within the whole fiscal system. Thus, the regressive nature of water and certain energy taxes may be acceptable, because compensatory measures already exist in the fiscal system.

Let us change the approach to distributional issues. Should the tax be imposed on the taxpayer if the tax law so determines and no exceptions to it are allowed?[39] In environmental taxation this issue is especially related to the adjustment of taxes. We may claim that it has special significance in respect of environmental taxes, because the financial burden caused by these taxes may be heavy on polluters in particular in comparison with direct regulation, and because environmental taxes are levied irrespective of the financial position of the taxpayers.[40]

A negative attitude towards the adjustment of taxes can be justified to some extent by the equal tax treatment of taxpayers. For instance, if a tax adjustment is granted easily in VAT and in corporate income taxation, it would bias the competitive position between taxpayers. A further argument against tax adjustment is the fact that if someone avoids taxes, others then have to pay more to achieve the desired revenue goal. In addition, the flexible application of a tax adjustment could make taxation more vulnerable to such a phenomenon, which in direct regulation is usually called regulatory capture. Tax adjustment has to be the exception or otherwise a large share of taxpayers will require exemptions or relief from taxes.

Some additional arguments may be presented particularly in respect of regulatory taxes. The purpose of fiscal taxes is to sustain the tax base, and it is therefore in the interests of the legislator that the tax does not bankrupt the taxpayers. The matter is somewhat different in regulatory taxation. In some cases, the purpose is to erode the tax base totally, as in the case of a tax on environmentally damaging products, which aims at a total shift to the consumption of benign products. In any case, the primary purpose of incentive environmental taxes is to achieve the desired environmental policy goals, even if it results in such things as the shutdown of some older plants. Consequently, and because the threat to close down a polluting factory is unthinkable and not credible in direct regulation, some researchers have recommended the adoption of environmental taxes.[41] An argument advocating the adjustment of environmental taxes is the polluter-pays principle, which allows subsidies in environmental policy if they are related to industries, areas and plants where severe difficulties would occur. This approach makes it possible to include other policy interests, such as employment considerations in environmental taxation. The negative side of the coin is that environmental policy targets may be obscured as a result.

Because of the economic burden created by environmental taxes, it has been recommended that a tax adjustment should be possible if the tax fundamentally threatens the position of a polluter in relation to his or her competitors. At the same time no general tax adjustment should be possible. A tax adjustment is also deemed applicable when the international competitiveness of some domestic industries is threatened. In this sense, the adjustment can be considered to be *ex post* tax relief for the open sector.[42] In adjusting environmental taxes it has also been shown that polluters may be in an unequal position concerning their possibilities of reducing pollution. For instance, when a new tax law is enacted some polluters can immediately take measures to reduce effluents and their tax burden, whereas others can only take measures after a few years. These considerations are impossible to take into account *ex ante*, which cause inequality across polluters. Hence, the transitional problems and the minimization of transitory costs support the need for incorporating adjustment provisions into the environmental tax laws.

Another point of view indicates that tax adjustment should be possible if no other technical measures exist to limit pollution. For instance, if it is impossible to reduce nitrogen oxide emissions below a given level, adjustment provisions would be applicable. The tax adjustment in this case appears to be moderate, but at the same time it leads to similar problems in environmental taxation, which are familiar in direct regulation. Given the asymmetrical information between the regulator and regulatees, authorities do not know with any certainty when technical measures exist to limit pollution.

Advocates of tax adjustment legitimate the procedure by means of the way environmental tax laws are implemented. Because environmental taxes are quite often imposed as a component in a mixed tax, it would be inconsistent not to apply similar rules both to the regulatory and fiscal components of the tax. Equally inconsistent would be to accept a tax adjustment with respect to mixed-type taxes but not to pure environmental taxes.

Finally, attention should be paid to the fact that tax adjustment is not a suitable way to remedy grievances in legislation. In other words, tax adjustment provisions should be applied only in individual cases, not as a policy instrument. According to the legality principle, policy instruments in taxation should be enacted by law. There are numerous reasons for not adjusting environmental taxes. Therefore, affordability considerations should be primarily taken into account *ex ante*. For instance, selective revenue recycling, employing redistributive environmental taxes and the use of a progressive timetable in setting the environmental tax rate are a potential means for achieving this.

NOTES

1   See Bohm (1994), 91.
2   See OECD (1995), 76, and Whitehouse (1996), 75.
3   TemaNord 1996:568, 33.
4   See TemaNord 1996:568, 31–32.
5   See SOU 1990:59, 176 and 435.
6   See Määttä (1997), 97 ff.

7   See Johnson, McKay and Smith (1990), 2.
8   See COM(96) 546 final, 9.
9   See Bohm and Russell (1985), 438.
10 See Gren (1996), 180 and 190.
11 See TemaNord 1996:568, 75.
12 See OECD (1993), 95.
13 See Smith (1997), 29, and Spackman (1997), 29.
14 Cf. Paulus (1995), 48.
15 See von Weitzäcker and Jesinghaus (1992), 58, and Oosterhuis and de Savornin Lohman (1994), 37.
16 See von Weitzäcker and Jesinghaus (1992), 58.
17 See Oosterhuis and de Savornin Lohman (1994), 37.
18 See OECD (1988), 54.
19 OECD (1993), 54.
20 See Cnossen (1992), 132.
21 OECD (1988), 58, and Cnossen (1992), 132.
22 Cnossen and Vollebergh (1992), 29.
23 See SOU 1989:35, 315.
24 OECD (1988), 58.
25 Cnossen (1977), 3.
26 Terra (1988), 38.
27 See Määttä (2004), 69 ff.
28 See Heyndels and Smolders (1995), 127 ff.
29 See Buchanan (1967), 132, and Goetz (1977), 177–178.
30 See Messere (1993), 112.
31 On double-dividend gain, see Terkla (1984), 107 ff, Goulder (1995), 157 ff, and McCoy (1997), 201 ff.
32 See Bovenberg (1999), 421 ff.
33 Määttä (1999a), 327.
34 See Musgrave and Musgrave (1989), 215.
35 See Messere (1993), 436.
36 See Määttä (1997), 216–218.
37 See von Weitzäcker and Jesinghaus (1992), 60.
38 See Heineken (2003), 189 ff.
39 See Määttä (1997), 239–243.
40 See SOU 1993:118, 89.
41 See White (1976), 113.
42 See SOU 1993:118, 89–90.

8. Concluding Remarks

8.1 CONCEPTUAL ISSUES

Even though defining the scope of environmental taxes is inevitably imprecise, some kind of conceptual framework is necessary. The starting point has been that there is not only one but several types of environmental tax.

Incentive environmental taxes are created in order to guide the behaviour of polluters, whereas their revenues are of secondary importance. In principle, the tax level is determined by the desired goal of pollution reduction or a reduction in the use of natural resources. On the other hand, the tax level has not always been determined in such a manner.

Financing environmental taxes are desirable as sources of revenue for funding environmental protection measures. The tax level is determined, in principle, by the revenue need for these measures and the proceeds for them are earmarked.

Fiscal environmental taxes are taxes which are primarily aimed at generating revenue but which may have significant positive effects on the environment. Thus, the primary purpose of fiscal environmental taxes deviates from incentive environmental taxes. The proceeds from fiscal environmental taxes are not earmarked like those from financing environmental taxes.

One legal and conceptual difficulty is to draw the borderline between environmental taxes and environmental charges precisely. Taxes are defined briefly as unrequited payments in which benefits provided by governments to taxpayers are not normally in proportion to their payment. By definition, levying environmental charges requires the existence of a public service providing benefits to users or customers. Moreover, environmental charges can cover total expenditures from producing services but nothing more.

From the instrumental point of view, economists have commonly recommended that effluent taxes are the best way to implement environmental taxes. Effluent taxes can be defined as taxes paid on discharges into the environment. Nevertheless, product taxes are in practice a common form of environmental taxes. They may be based, for instance, on the weight of the product or its environmentally detrimental characteristics. Waste taxes are usually levied when waste is delivered to the waste sites.

Environmental taxes are not applied alone. Mixed systems are characteristic of environmental regulation with or without environmental taxes. Therefore, it is very important to recognize the position of environmental taxes. Of course, they may be independent in nature, where regulation is based completely or mainly on environmental tax. However, the usual situation is that environmental taxes are complementary in nature. At the same time, it should be noted that complementary environmental taxes vary from one case to another. In relation to direct regulation, incentive environmental taxes may be reinforcing or preparatory in nature. Moreover, there are mixed systems which consist of economic instruments, such as tax-cum-subsidy schemes.

8.2 THEORY IS THEORY AND PRACTICE IS PRACTICE

The Buchanan–Tullock theorem takes into account one relevant factor behind the development of environmental tax policy – the influence of regulatees on regulators. In other words, it reminds us of the significance of lobbying. We should take seriously the possibility that interest groups exert strong pressure on the introduction and the design of environmental taxes. This phenomenon creates instability in environmental tax legislation, which is an essential pitfall concerning the regulatory function of these taxes. In this sense, there is a regulatory dilemma involving environmental taxes because business likes certainty, but, on the other hand, it will lobby against these taxes thereby creating uncertainty in the circumstances in which the business operates.

On the other hand, it is possible to criticize the theorem on many grounds, not least of which is the difficulty in explaining the growing use of environmental taxes. More generally, the theorem passes over a multiplicity of forces spurring the development of environmental tax policy. For instance, the rise of the environmentalists, environmental policy and tax policy considerations, administrative considerations, competitive disadvantages, successful examples of national environmental tax policy as well as general deregulation policy have been mentioned as reasons given for the development of environmental tax policy in the past three decades. Nevertheless, it is important to outline legitimacy strategies which can reduce the tensions between lobbies and the legislator, and, without endangering or minimizing the danger, the environmental effectiveness and efficiency properties of the taxes concerned. From this point of view, the interaction between legitimacy strategies and the normative theory of regulation should be noted.

Redistributive taxes and selective revenue recycling are in some cases good illustrations of legitimacy strategies. A progressive time schedule for setting environmental tax rates as well as other methods of progressive implementation may offer possibilities for improving the acceptability of taxes while at the same time reducing any adjustment costs. In addition to the legitimacy strategies mentioned in Chapter 3, we should remember the differentiated environmental taxation between the closed and open sector of the economy. Furthermore, providing adequate information for target groups as well as consulting with them can serve as legitimacy strategies. Finally, 'piggy-backing' environmental taxes onto the existing legislation has minimized administrative costs – and also the adjustment costs of both regulators and regulatees – paving the way for a more extensive use of environmental taxes.

A positive theory of regulation and administrative considerations may chiefly explain why actual environmental taxes are far from the 'textbook taxes' analysed by economists. For instance, only a quite small share of environmental taxes are effluent taxes, and furthermore, even these taxes are not always based on measured emissions due to the high costs involved. Another point of view is that in addition to their role as incentive taxes environmental taxes have been implemented as financing taxes, and in some circumstances it may even be preferable to do so. Furthermore, mixed systems have often been ignored in the discussion, despite their significant position in practice. Finally, it has been recommended that the iterative process should be applied in setting the rate of an incentive environmental tax. However, this process has been very rarely applied in practice. Its application has been avoided by gradually increasing the tax rates or by applying mixed systems. On the other hand, the legislator does not operate in a total 'information vacuum' and sometimes the estimation of the tax level has been correct the first time.

8.3 REGULATORY AND FISCAL TAXES

It has been stated that regulatory taxes are characterized by a legal paradox. On the one hand, such taxes deviate significantly in nature from conventional fiscal taxes. For instance, incentive environmental taxes act as preventive mechanisms, such as compensation for environmental damage or criminal law, and their primary goal is to improve the state of the environment and, thus, fiscal considerations are secondary. On the other hand, similar rules would apply to both regulatory taxes and fiscal taxes. Such an application is also appropriate from an environmental point of view.

The reasons for the dominant position of the continuity principle are manifold and vary somewhat case by case. However, some general arguments are briefly presented. First, an exact definition of regulatory taxes is almost impossible. No purely objective criteria can be found to define these taxes, and the definition is bound up with the goals of legislation, which are often indeterminate. The explicit and actual goals of tax legislation may also deviate from each other. Moreover, the goals of regulatory taxes are obscured because in practice there are so many departures from the 'ideal' regulatory taxes. For instance, certain activities are exempted from the tax even though they should be regulated. In these circumstances, any hope of making sharp distinctions in the legal treatment between fiscal and regulatory taxes is restricted.

Second, another essential reason for following the continuity principle relates to the legislative technique applied when regulatory taxes are enacted. This especially concerns those regulatory taxes which are incorporated into existing fiscal taxes. Consistency and administrative considerations support the application of similar rules for both the fiscal and regulatory components of these mixed taxes. On the other hand, when regulatory taxes are implemented as separate laws, it would be inconsistent not to apply similar 'rules of the game' to them as are applied to regulatory tax components in mixed taxes. In addition, product-related regulatory taxes are generally 'piggy-backed' onto the existing excise taxation procedure, which further streamlines regulatory and fiscal taxes.

Finally, the legal nature of regulatory taxes is obscured, in effect, because they may be used for revenue-raising purposes, that is to finance, in particular, a reduction of income taxes. On the other hand, there is a threat that certain new regulatory taxes, especially incentive environmental taxes, would go the way of alcohol and tobacco taxes: they become primarily revenue sources rather than mechanisms to change the conduct of regulatees.

All these issues are connected to the emergence of regulatory taxation. In short, regulatory taxes were not created in a vacuum, but their adoption has been closely linked to both the tax and regulatory legislation. Hence, it is only logical that the continuity principle should be dominant when the legal problems regarding regulatory taxes are examined. We should then note what North (1990) has written: 'Institutions typically change incrementally rather than in discontinuous fashion'.

These considerations do not mean that regulatory taxes could be adjusted to the legal system to preclude amendments to the existing legislation. For instance, incentive environmental taxes create pressures to revise the scope of motor vehicle and fuel taxation. It is incompatible with the regulatory nature of environmental taxes, for example, to exempt off-road use of vehicles from taxation if it causes pollution, and on the other hand, to tax such fuels which do not. This clearly demonstrates that regulatory tax may be a useful concept in legal policy-making even though its role in the interpretation of environmental tax laws and related legislation is minor.

8.4 INCENTIVE ENVIRONMENTAL TAXES

The nature of environmental problems is critical with respect to the viable design of incentive environmental taxes. However, one peculiar feature has been their uniform structure and level, even though they are often used to regulate non-uniformly mixed pollutants. Thus, administrative considerations have dominated the regulatory options adopted in practice.

From the standpoint of the environmental effectiveness point, compared to direct regulation, incentive environmental taxes should not be condemned as inappropriate measures. Direct regulation may have unpredictable effects on total pollution: under direct regulation flexible norms are often applied, compliance with direct regulation is not an 'all-or-nothing' decision, and direct regulation may be difficult to implement when the aim is only to reduce the consumption of certain products. In addition, an iterative process is not the only way to determine the correct level for an incentive environmental tax, which may help the introduction of these taxes.

The marginal tax rate is, of course, very important for the environmental effectiveness of incentive environmental taxes, but is not the only issue. For instance, the timetable for setting the incentive tax rate, the comprehensiveness of an incentive tax as well as the linkage between pollution and environmental tax must also be taken into account.

Cost-effectiveness has become an essential reason for legitimating incentive environmental taxes at the legislative level. However, it is by no means evident that incentive environmental taxes, in effect, would even approach the least-cost means of reducing pollution, since so many compromises are made to these taxes at the micro-policy level. For instance, the marginal tax rate may be so low that an environmental tax does not affect the behaviour of polluters; direct regulation may be a binding constraint in a mixed system at least for some of the polluters; the variability of tax rates among polluters for non-environmental reasons may also weaken cost-effectiveness; narrow-based environmental taxes pose distinct problems, because they may be directed at activities which make the reduction of pollution very expensive; the linkage between pollution and the tax level is also of great importance in this respect; shortcomings in technological flexibility are reflected as shortcomings in the cost-effectiveness of environmental taxes; finally, cost-effectiveness would be eroded by the unpredictability of tax treatment and tax legislation.

In short, there seems to be a gap between macro-policy and micro-policy levels in the role of cost-effectiveness. When incentive environmental taxes are compared with direct regulation, cost-effectiveness is one of the main arguments supporting the introduction of a tax option as opposed to tightening direct regulation. However, at the micro-policy level, where the tax is designed, cost-effectiveness loses much of its power as a regulatory standard. In this respect, cost-effectiveness has been used – at least to some extent – as an illusory justification for incentive environmental taxes. Incentive environmental taxes have also been justified by another efficiency property, dynamic efficiency. However, dynamic efficiency is clearly an ambiguous source of legitimation for incentive environmental taxes. For instance, little evidence has been found to suggest that environmental taxes have stimulated innovations in pollution abatement. In practice, the promotion of dynamic efficiency may face many of the same pitfalls as the promotion of cost-effectiveness. The dynamic efficiency of incentive environmental taxes has also become a controversial criterion in environmental tax literature. The counter-argument has been that the tax burden leaves firms with fewer resources for R&D and, thus, the creation of cleaner methods of production may be slower than under direct regulation. In addition, technological development also has another side. It has paved the way for some new environmental taxes. For instance, one factor that will have a crucial impact on the application of environmental taxes is the technology of monitoring. As monitoring costs go down, the use of mechanisms such as direct effluent taxes can be expected to rise.

8.5 FINANCING ENVIRONMENTAL TAXES

Financing environmental taxes should not be ignored when potential candidates for environmental protection and financing are sought, even though there are also several limitations on the application of these taxes. Financing environmental taxes may be more appropriate and even more cost-effective tools in certain circumstances than incentive environmental taxes. Particularly in cases where reducing the detrimental effects of the environmental problem cannot take place most inexpensively at the source of pollution, financing environmental tax may prove to be an appropriate solution. This shows how important it is to distinguish between financing and incentive environmental taxes, a distinction which is often omitted or neglected. On the other hand, financing environmental taxes partly illustrate the fact that distinctions between different instruments in environmental policy are not unambiguous. For instance, tax refund systems for car hulks might just as well be labelled financing environmental taxes as deposit refund systems.

According to the conventional view in public economics, earmarking is a source of inefficiency in allocating proceeds to spending needs. However, the earmarking of environmental tax proceeds should not be condemned outright as an improper regulatory option. Earmarking is legitimate particularly with respect to financing environmental taxes, even though it cannot be recommended in the case of incentive environmental taxes. The criticism levelled against earmarking proceeds from environmental taxes has been too categorical and ignores the minor fiscal importance of financing taxes in practice and the different procedures by which tax proceeds can be earmarked. On the other hand, improving the acceptability of environmental taxes does not usually offer sufficient grounds alone for earmarking the proceeds from those taxes.

In addition, financing environmental taxes may sometimes provide a more appropriate way to finance the environmental protection measures than proceeds from income tax or VAT. For instance, regulatory provisions could be incorporated into financing environmental taxes, but it is impossible to affect the revenue needs in environmental programmes if the revenues are generated by income tax or VAT. On the other hand, administrative considerations as well as vulnerability to inappropriate tax avoidance may limit the scope for applying financing environmental taxes as a source of revenue in environmental policy.

8.6 ENVIRONMENTAL TAXES FROM THE FISCAL POINT OF VIEW

Fiscal considerations have been regarded as important within the context of environmental taxes. For instance, de Savornin Lohman (1994) has written that the Scandinavian countries have experienced a 'legitimacy crisis' over income taxation, stimulating them to go for environmental taxation as a financing alternative. Similarly, Andersen (1995) has stressed that the fiscal crisis of the Scandinavian welfare states is an essential reason for the adoption of environmental taxes.

We can, however, claim that the discussion concerning the (potential) fiscal importance of environmental taxes has been biased. In effect, environmental taxes which can be classified as functionally equivalent to environmental policy tools are mainly non-revenue-generating taxes or taxes which generate very small proceeds. Moreover, the maximum revenue potential of these taxes is generally very limited. Hence, most incentive environmental taxes have to be evaluated solely as environmental policy instruments since their revenue is a remainder, and more specifically a minor remainder.

With regard to very small taxes, generating proceeds of less than 0.1 per cent of total tax proceeds, revenue-raising and environmental objectives may contradict each other. If tax revenues from incentive environmental taxes are earmarked for special purposes, a problem arises: when should revenue needs take precedence and when the desired incentive impact? Both of these goals are attainable only by chance, as the Tinbergen rule indicates. Similar problems may arise when a financing environmental tax is directed at an item which may react sensitively to the tax.

The conflict between environmental and fiscal objectives, however, mainly concentrates on such taxes as the carbon tax, the water tax and especially on fiscal environmental taxes. What are our possibilities of changing the tax mix by means of environmental taxes? What are the pros and cons of these taxes compared to conventional fiscal taxes involving fiscal stability and fiscal flexibility? What is the role of fiscal illusion and what needs do environmental taxes create for the development of other parts of the tax legislation?

There has been relatively little scope for changing the tax mix through the use of environmental taxes, particularly in respect of reducing income tax. First, selective revenue recycling has been of importance as a legitimacy strategy, since other energy taxes have been reduced due to the introduction of carbon tax or taxes on some specific sector have been reduced to counterbalance the tax burden created by a new environmental tax. In other words, selective revenue recycling substantially reduces the margin for general revenue recycling. Second, a topic which has been ignored in the tax policy discussion is that environmental taxes are, in effect, needed to finance a reduction in other excise duties, in particular tobacco and alcohol taxes. Third, if we wish to design fiscal environmental taxes so that they serve environmental policy goals in an appropriate fashion, this does not necessarily mean higher tax rates but restructured tax provisions and some totally new tax institutions. Finally, all environmental taxes are fiscally narrow-based taxes. Thus, the rate of these taxes has to be much higher than the tax rates of broad-based taxes, such as VAT, in order for them to generate significant proceeds. However, very high tax rates will make environmental taxes vulnerable to international tax competition. In other words, cross-border shopping may increase substantially and the relocation effect may become a reality. In addition, high tax rates may erode the tax base 'domestically': taxable activities may decrease at some stage more than the tax rate increases and, thus, tax proceeds will diminish.

Bibliography

Aarnio, Aulis (1978), *Mitä lainoppi on?* (What is Legal Dogmatics?), Helsinki: Tammi.

Aarnio, Aulis (1986), *The Rational as Reasonable*, Dordrecht: Kluwer Academic Publishers.

Andersen, Mikael Skou (1994), *Governance by Green Taxes: Making Pollution Prevention Pay*, Manchester and New York: Manchester University Press.

Andersen, Mikael Skou (1995), 'The Use of Economic Instruments for Environmental Policy: A Half Hearted Affair', in TemaNord 1995:588, *Sustainable Patterns of Consumption and Production*, Nordic Council of Ministers, pp. 55–69.

Andersen, Mikael Skou (2003), 'CO_2 Taxation in the Nordic Countries: Results and Methodological Caveats', in Janet Milne, Kurt Deketelaere, Larry Kreiser and Hope Ashiabor (eds), *Critical Issues in Environmental Taxation: International and Comparative Perspectives*, vol. I, Richmond, UK: Richmond, pp. 163–174.

Anderson, Frederick R., Kneese, Allen V., Reed, Phillip D., Taylor, Serge and Stevenson, Russel B. (1977), *Environmental Improvement Through Economic Incentives,* Baltimore and London: The Johns Hopkins University Press..

Barde, Jean-Phillippe (1997), 'Environmental Taxation: Experience in OECD Countries', in Tim O'Riordan (ed.), *Ecotaxation,* London: Earthscan Publications, pp. 223–245.

Barde, Jean-Philippe and Opschoor, Johannes Baptist (1994), 'From Stick to Carrot in the Environment', *The OECD Observer*, 186, 23–27.

Barde, Jean-Philippe and Owens, Jeffrey (1993), 'The Greening of Taxation', *The OECD Observer*, 182, 27–30.

Barde, Jean-Philippe and Owens, Jeffrey (1996), 'The Evolution of Eco-taxes', *The OECD Observer*, 198, 11–16.

Barde, Jean-Philippe and Smith, Stephen (1997), 'Do Economic Instruments Help the Environment?', *The OECD Observer*, 204, 22–26.

Barker, Terry (1993), 'The Carbon Tax: Economic and Policy Issues', in Carlo Carraro and Domenico Siniscalco (eds), *The European Carbon Tax: An Economic Assessment*, Dordrecht, Boston and London: Kluwer Academic, pp. 239–254.

Barthold, Thomas A. (1994), 'Issues in the Design of Environmental Excise Taxes', *Journal of Economic Perspectives*, 8 (1), 133–151.

Baumol, W.J. and Oates, W.E. (1971), 'The Use of Standards and Prices for Protection of Environment', *Swedish Journal of Economics*, 73 (1), 42–54.

Baumol, William J. and Oates, Wallace E. (1988), *The Theory of Environmental Policy*, 2nd ed., Cambridge: Cambridge University Press.

Bohm, Peter (1994), 'Environment and Taxation: The Case of Sweden', in OECD Documents, *Environment and Taxation: The Cases of the Netherlands, Sweden and the United States*, Paris, pp. 51–101.

Bohm, Peter and Russell, Clifford S. (1985), 'Comparative Analysis of Alternative Policy Measures', in A.V. Kneese and J.L. Sweeney (eds), *Handbook of Natural Resources and Energy Economics*, vol. I, Amsterdam: Elsevier Science Publishers B.V., pp. 395–460.

Bovenberg, A.L. (1999), 'Green Tax Reforms and the Double Dividend: An Updated Reader's Guide', *International Tax and Public Finance*, 421–443.

Bracewell-Milnes, Barry (1992), 'Taxation and the Environment', *Intertax*, 2, 154–155.

Bregha, Francois and Moffet, John (1995), 'Sustainable Development and Budget Reform', in Robert Gale, Stephan Barg, with Alexander Gillies (eds), *Green Budget Reform: An International Casebook of Leading Practices*, London: Earthscan Publications Ltd., pp. 346–358.

Brown, Gardner M. Jr. and Johnson, Ralph (1984), 'Pollution Control by Effluent Charges: It Works in the Federal Republic of Germany, Why Not in the U.S.?' *Natural Resources Journal*, 24, 929–966.

Buchanan, James M. (1967), *Public Finance in Democratic Process: Fiscal Institutions and Individual Choice*, Berkeley, CA: University of North Carolina Press.

Buchanan, James M. and Tullock, Gordon (1975), 'Polluters' Profits and Political Response: Direct Controls Versus Taxes', *The American Economic Review*, 65, 139–147.

Buchanan, James M. and Tullock, Gordon (1976), 'Polluters' Profits and Political Response: Direct Controls Versus Taxes: Reply', *The American Economic Review*, 66, 983–984.

van Calster, Geert (2003), 'Topsy-turvy: The European Court of Justice and Border (Energy) Tax Adjustments: Should the World Trade Organization Follow Suit?', in Janet Milne, Kurt Deketelaere, Larry Kreiser and Hope Ashiabor (eds), *Critical Issues in Environmental Taxation: International and Comparative Perspectives*, vol. I, Richmond, UK: Richmond, pp. 311–341.

Cnossen, Sijbren (1977), *Excise Systems: A Global Study of the Selective Taxation of Goods and Services*, Baltimore and London: The John Hopkins University Press.

Cnossen, Sijbren (1992), 'Intrigues Around the Tobacco Excise in the European Community', *Intertax 2*, 127–137.

Cnossen, Sijbren and Vollebergh, Herman R.J. (1992), 'Toward a Global Excise on Carbon', *National Tax Journal*, 23–36.

Coase, R.H. (1960), 'The Problem of Social Cost', *Journal of Law and Economics*, 3, 1–44.

Coase, R.H. (1988), *The Firm, the Market and the Law*, Chicago and London: The University of Chicago Press.

Coelho, P. (1976), 'Polluters, Profits and Political Response: Direct Control Versus Taxes: Comment', *The American Economic Review*, 66, 976–978.

Commission of the European Communities (1996), 'Taxation in the European Union', *Report on the Development of Tax Systems*, COM(96) 546 final, Brussels 22.10.1996.

Commission of the European Communities (1997), 'Communication from the Commission', *Environmental Taxes and Charges in the Single Market*, COM(97) 9 final, Brussels, 26.03.1997.

Convery, Frank J. and Rooney, Shenagh (1996), 'Making Markets Work for the Economy and the Environment: Lessons from Experience in Greece, Ireland, Portugal and Spain', in *Environmental Taxes & Charges: National Experiences & Plans*, papers from the Dublin Workshop, 'European Foundation for the

Improvement of Living and Working Conditions', Luxembourg: Office for Official Publications of the European Communities, pp. 15–43.

Copeland, Brian R. (1991), 'International Trade in Waste Products in the Presence of Illegal Disposal', *Journal of Environmental Economics and Management*, 20, 143–162.

de Clercq, Marc (1994), 'The Political Economy of Green Taxes: The Belgian Experience', in TemaNord 1994:647, *Economic Instruments in Environmental Policy – in a Europe Without Border Control*, Nordic Council of Ministers, Copenhagen, pp. 44–59.

de Clercq, Marc (1996), 'The Implementation of Green Product Taxes: The Belgian Experience', in *Environmental Taxes & Charges: National Experiences & Plans*, papers from the Dublin Workshop, 'European Foundation for the Improvement of Living and Working Conditions', Luxembourg: Office for Official Publications of the European Communities, pp. 45–66.

de Grauwe, Paul (1993), 'Economic Instruments in EC Environmental Policy', Centre for European Policy Studies, *Working Party Report No. 8*.

Deketelaere, Kurt (1993), 'The European Environmental Policy and the Use of Market-based Instruments', *ELSA Law Review*, 2, 45–67.

Deketelaere, Kurt (1995), 'Towards European Environmental Tax Law: Greenspeak', in Filip Abraham, Kurt Deketelaere and Jules Stuyck (eds), *Recent Economic and Legal Developments in European Environmental Policy: Generale Bank Lectures 1993–1994*, Leuwen: Leuwen University Press, pp. 169–194.

de Savornin Lohman, Lex (1994), 'Economic Incentives in Environmental Policy: Why are They White Ravens?', in J.B. Opschoor and R.K. Turner (eds), *Economic Incentives and Environmental Policies: Principles and Practice*, Dordrecht, Boston and London: Kluwer Academic , pp. 55–67.

Dewees, D. (1983), 'Instrument Choice in Environmental Policy', *Economic Inquiry*, XXI, 53–71.

Driesen, David M. (2003), 'Why Pollution Taxes Cannot Replace Command and Control Regulation (But Should Have a Bright Future Nonetheless)', in Janet Milne, Kurt Deketelaere, Larry Kreiser and Hope Ashiabor (eds), *Critical Issues in Environmental Taxation: International and Comparative Perspectives*, vol. I, Richmond, UK: Richmond, pp. 51–60.

Ds. 1994:33, *Så fungerar miljöskatter* (How Environmental Taxes Work), ministry report, Stockholm, Sweden.

Ekins, Paul (1996), 'Environmental Taxes & Charges: National Experiences & Plans', *Report of the European Workshop held at Dublin* on 7-8 February 1996, European Foundation for the Improvement of Living and Working Conditions. Luxembourg: Office for Official Publications of the European Communities.

European Environment Agency (1996), *Environmental Taxes: Implementation and Environmental Effectiveness,* Copenhagen.

Faure, Michael and Stefan Ubachs (2003), 'Comparative Benefits and Optimal Use of Environmental Taxes', in Janet Milne, Kurt Deketelaere, Larry Kreiser and Hope Ashiabor (eds), *Critical Issues in Environmental Taxation: International and Comparative Perspectives*, vol. I, Richmond, UK: Richmond, pp. 27–49.

Faure, Michael, Vervaele, John and Weale, Albert (1994), 'Introduction', in Michael Faure, John Vervaele and Albert Weale (eds), *Environmental Standards in the European Union in an Interdisciplinary Framework*, Antwerpen Apeldoorn: MAKLU Uitgevers, pp. 5–9.

Gale, Robert and Barg, Stephan R. (1995), 'The Greening of Budgets: The Choice of Governing Instrument', in Robert Gale, Stephan Barg with Alexander Gillies (eds), *Green Budget Reform: An International Casebook of Leading Practices*, London: Earthscan Publications, pp. 1–27.

Godard, Olivier (1993), 'Taxes', in OECD, *International Economic Instruments and Climate Change*, Paris, pp. 43–101.

Goetz, Charles J. (1977), 'Fiscal Illusion in State and Local Finance', in Thomas E. Borcherding (ed.), *Budgets and Bureaucrats: The Structures of Government Growth*, Durham, NC: Duke Government Press, pp. 176–187.

Goulder, Lawrence H. (1995), 'Environmental Taxation and the Double Dividend: A Reader's Guide', *International Tax and Public Finance*, 157–183.

Grabitz, Eberhard and Zacker, Christian (1989), 'Scope for Action by the EC Member States for the Improvement of Environmental Protection Under EEC Law: The Example of Environmental Taxes and Subsidies', *Common Market Law Review*, 26, 423–447.

Gren, Ing-Marie (1996), 'Intäkter och miljövinster av skatter på handelsgödsel och bekämpningsmedel', in SOU 1996:117, *Expertrapporter från Skatteväxlingskommitten*, Stockholm, pp. 167–203.

Hahn, Robert W. (1989), *A Primer on Environmental Policy Design*, London, Paris, New York and Melbourne: Harwood Academic.

Hahn, R.W. (1990), 'The Political Economy of Environmental Regulation: Towards a Unifying Framework', *Public Choice*, 21–47.

Hahn, Robert W. and Stavins, Robert N. (1992), 'Economic Incentives for Environmental Protection: Integrating Theory and Practice', *The American Economic Review*, 82 (2), 464–469.

Heineken, Kees A. (2003), 'The History of the Dutch Regulatory Energy Tax: How the Dutch Introduced and Expanded a Tax on Small-scale Energy Use', in Janet Milne, Kurt Deketelaere, Larry Kreiser and Hope Ashiabor (eds.), *Critical Issues in Environmental Taxation: International and Comparative Perspectives*, vol. I, Richmond, UK: Richmond, pp. 189–225.

Helm, Dieter and Pearce, David (1990), 'The Assessment: Economic Policy Towards the Environment', *Oxford Review of Economic Policy*, 6 (1), 1–16.

Heyndels, B. and Smolders, C. (1995), 'Tax Complexity and Fiscal Illusion', *Public Choice*, 85 (1–2), 127–141.

Hourcade, Jean Charles and Baron, Richard (1993), 'Tradeable Permits', in OECD, *International Economic Instruments and Climate Change*, Paris, pp. 11–42.

Huppes, Gjalt and Kagan, Robert A. (1989), 'Market-Oriented Regulation of Environmental Problems in the Netherlands', *Law & Policy*, 11 (2), 215–239.

IEA (1993), *Taxing Energy: Why and How*, Paris.

International Fiscal Association (1995), *Environmental Taxes and Charges*, proceedings of a seminar held in Florence, Italy in 1993 during the 47th Congress of the International Fiscal Association, The Hague, London and Boston.

Jacobs, Michael (1991), *The Green Economy: Environment, Sustainable Development and the Politics of the Future*, London: Pluto Press.

Jaffe, Adam B., Peterson, Steven R., Portney, Paul R. and Stavins Robert N. (1995), 'Environmental Regulation and the Competitiveness of U.S. Manufacturing: What Does the Evidence Tell Us?', *Journal of Economic Literature*, 132–163.

Johnson, Paul, McKay, Steve and Smith, Stephen (1990), *The Distributional Consequences of Environmental Taxes*, IFS Commentary 23, London: The Institute for Fiscal Studies.

Klami, Hannu Tapani (1977), *Oikeudellisen sääntelyn yleinen teoria* (General Theory of Legal Regulation. Publication of the Department of Private Law at the

University of Turku), Turun yliopiston yksityisoikeuden laitoksen julkaisuja 12, 1977, Turku.

Km. 1993:35. *Ympäristötaloustoimikunnan mietintö*, (The Report of the Environment Economics Committee), Helsinki.

Kneese, A. and Schultze, C. (1975), *Pollution, Prices and Public Policy*, Washington, DC: The Brookings Institution.

Määttä, Kalle (1997), *Environmental Taxes: From an Economic Idea to a Legal Institution*, Jyväskylä: Kauppakaari Oy. Finnish Lawyers' Publishing.

Määttä, Kalle (1999), 'Environmental Versus Fiscal Considerations in Taxing Energy', *International Journal of Global Energy Issues*, 319–331.

Määttä, Kalle (2001), *Regulatory Reform and Innovations: Whether to Trust Invisible Hand to Use Visible One?*, Sitra report series 10, Helsinki.

Määttä, Kalle (2002), 'Regulatory Taxes: Theoretical Considerations', in Michael Faure, Jan Smits and Hildegard Schneider (eds), *Towards a European Ius Commune in Legal Education and Research*, Antwerpen Groningen: Intersentia Uitgevers, pp. 155–168.

Määttä, Kalle (2003), 'Finnish Energy Taxation: How Well Has It Worked?', in Janet Milne, Kurt Deketelaere, Larry Kreiser and Hope Ashiabor (eds), *Critical Issues in Environmental Taxation: International and Comparative Perspectives*, vol. I, Richmond, UK: Richmond, pp. 175–188.

Määttä, Kalle (2004), 'Fiscal Illusion and Environmental Taxes in Practice', in Adam Budnikowski, Maciej Cygler and Elzbieta Czarny (eds), *Integration in the Globalising World Economy*, Warszawa, pp. 69–78.

Main, Robert S. and Baird, Charles W. (1976), 'Polluters, Profits and Political Response: Direct Control Versus Taxes: Comment', *The American Economic Review*, 66, 979–980.

Majocchi Alberto and Missaglia, Marco (2003), 'Environmental Taxes and Border Tax Adjustments: An Economic Assessment', in Janet Milne, Kurt Deketelaere, Larry Kreiser and Hope Ashiabor (eds), *Critical Issues in Environmental Taxation: International and Comparative Perspectives*, vol. I, Richmond, UK: Richmond, pp. 343–362.

Mäler, Karl-Göran (1984), 'Nya ekonomiska styrmedel i miljöpolitiken' (New Economic Instruments in Environmental Policy), *Ekonomisk Debatt*, 442–450.

Marquand, J.M. (1981), 'An Economist's View of Pollution Charges as Regulatory Instruments', in John A. Butlin (ed.), *The Economics of Environmental and Natural Resources Policy*, Boulder, CO: Westview Press, pp. 153–160.

McCoy, Daniel (1997), 'Reflections on the Double Dividend Debate', in Tim O'Riordan (ed.), *Ecotaxation*, London: Earthscan Publications, pp. 201–214.

Meade, J.E. (1973), *The Theory of Economic Externalities: The Control of Environmental Pollution and Similar Social Costs*, Geneva: Sijthoff.

Meade, J.E. (1978), *The Structure and Reform of Direct Taxation*, report of a Committee chaired by Professor J.E. Meade, The Institute for Fiscal Studies, London.

Medhurst, James (1993), 'Environmental Costs and Industry Competitiveness', in OECD, *Environmental Policies and Industrial Competitiveness*, Paris, pp. 37–47.

Messere, K.C. (1993), *Tax Policy in OECD Countries. Choices and Conflicts*, Amsterdam: IBFD Publications BV.

Milne, Janet E. (2003), 'Environmental Taxation: Why Theory Matters', in Janet Milne, Kurt Deketelaere, Larry Kreiser and Hope Ashiabor (eds), *Critical Issues in Environmental Taxation: International and Comparative Perspectives*, vol. I, Richmond, UK: Richmond, pp. 3–26.

Musgrave, Richard A. and Musgrave, Peggy B. (1989), *Public Finance in Theory and Practice*, 5th ed., New-York: McGraw-Hill.
Nichols, A.L. (1984), *Targeting Economic Incentives for Environmental Protection*, Cambridge, MA: MIT Press.
North, Douglass C. (1990), *Institutions, Institutional Change and Economic Performance*, Cambridge: Cambridge University Press.
NOU 1992:3, *Mot en mer kostnadseffektiv miljöpolitik i 1990-årene: Prinsipper og forslag til bedre prising av miljöet*, (Toward More Cost-Effective Environmental Policy in the 1990s. Principles and Proposals for Better Pricing of the Environment, Green Tax Commission, Norway), Oslo.
Oates, W.E. (1994), 'Environment and Taxation: The Case of the United States' in OECD Documents, *Environment and Taxation: The Cases of the Netherlands, Sweden and the United States*, Paris, 103–143.
OECD (1975), *The Polluter Pays Principle: Definition, Analysis and Implementation*, Paris.
OECD (1980), *Pollution Charges in Practice*, Paris.
OECD (1984), *Tax Expenditures: A Review of the Issues and Country Practices*, report by the Committee on Fiscal Affairs, Paris.
OECD (1985), *Environment and Economics*, Paris.
OECD (1988), *Taxing Consumption*, Paris.
OECD (1989), *Agricultural and Environmental Policies: Opportunities for Integration*, Paris.
OECD (1991), *Environmental Policy: How to Apply Economic Instruments*, Paris.
OECD (1993), *Taxation and the Environment: Complementary Policies*, Paris.
OECD (1994), *Managing the Environment: The Role of Economic Instruments*, Paris.
OECD (1995), *Environmental Taxes in OECD Countries*, Paris.
OECD (1996), *Implementation Strategies for Environmental Taxes*, Paris.
OECD (1997), *Evaluating Economic Instruments for Environmental Policy*, Paris.
OECD (1999), *Behavioural Responses to Environmentally-related Taxes*, Paris.
OECD (2001), *Environmentally Related Taxes in OECD Countries: Issues and Strategies*, Paris.
Ogus, Anthony (1994), *Regulation: Legal Form and Economic Theory*, Oxford: Clarendon Press.
Ogus, Anthony I. (2001), *Regulation, Economics and the Law*, Cheltenham, UK and Northampton, MA, USA: Edward Elgar.
Olivecrona, Christina (1995), 'The Nitrogen Oxide Charge on Energy Production in Sweden', in Robert Gale and Stephan Barg with Alexander Gillies (eds), *Green Budget Reform: An International Casebook of Leading Practices*, London: Earthscan Publications, pp. 163–172.
Oosterhuis, F.H. and de Savornin Lohman, A.F. (1994), 'Environment and Taxation: The Case of the Netherlands', in OECD Documents, *Environment and Taxation: The Cases of the Netherlands, Sweden and the United States*, Paris, pp. 7–50.
Opschoor, J.B. and Vos, H.B. (1989), *Economic Instruments for Environmental Protection*, Paris.
Paulus, Aggie (1995), *The Feasibility of Ecological Taxation*, Antwerpen Appeldoorn: MAKLU Uitgivers.
Pearce, D.W. and Turner, R.K. (1990), *Economics of Natural Resources and the Environment*, Baltimore: The John Hopkins University Press.
Pearson, Mark and Smith, Stephen (1991), *The European Carbon Tax: An Assessment of the European Commission's Proposals*, London: The Institute for Fiscal Studies.

Pechman, Joseph A. (1987), *Federal Tax Policy*, New York: Brookings Institution Press.

Pezzey, John (1988), 'Market Mechanisms of Pollution Control: "Polluter Pays", Economic and Practical Aspects', in R. Kerry Turner (ed.), *Sustainable Environmental Management: Principles and Practice*, London: Belhaven Press, pp. 190–242.

Pezzey, John (1992), 'The Symmetry Between Controlling Pollution by Price and Controlling it by Quantity', *Canadian Journal of Economics*, 983–991.

Piacentino, Diego (1994), 'Carbon Taxation and Global Warming: Domestic Policy Aspects', in J.B. Opschoor and R.K. Turner (eds), *Economic Incentives and Environmental Policies: Principles and Practice*, Dordrecht, Boston and London: Kluwer Academic, pp. 113–128.

Pigou, A.C. (1932), *The Economics of Welfare*, 4th ed., London: Macmillan.

Pittevils, Ivan (1996), 'Ecotaxes on Products in Belgium: The Need for a Proper Point of Imposition', in *Environmental Taxes & Charges: National Experiences & Plans*, papers from the Dublin Workshop, 'European Foundation for the Improvement of Living and Working Conditions', Luxembourg: Office for Official Publications of the European Communities, pp. 201–209.

Posner, Richard A. (1995), *Overcoming Law*, Cambridge, MA and London, UK: Harvard University Press.

Poterba, James M. (1991), 'Tax Policy to Combat Global Warming: On Designing a Carbon Tax', in R. Dornbusch and J. Poterba (eds), *Global Warming: Economic Policy Responses*, Cambridge, MA: The MIT Press, pp. 71–98.

Poterba, James M. (1993), 'Global Warming Policy: A Public Finance Perspective', *Journal of Economic Perspectives*, 7 (4), 47–63.

Puviani, Amilcare (1897), *Teoria della illusione nelle entrate publicie*, Perugia: Benucci.

Puviani, Amilcare (1903), *Teoria della illusione finangiaria*, Palermo: Sandron. Instituto Editoriale Internazionale.

Regan, D. (1972), 'The problem of social cost revisited', *Journal of Law and Economics*, 15, 427–437.

Rehbinder, Eckard (1993), 'Environmental Regulation Through Fiscal and Economic Incentives in a Federalist System', *Ecology Law Quarterly*, 20 (1), 57–83.

Richards, Kenneth R. (2003), 'The Instrument Choice Game: When Do Environmental Taxes Win?', in Janet Milne, Kurt Deketelaere, Larry Kreiser and Hope Ashiabor (eds), *Critical Issues in Environmental Taxation: International and Comparative Perspectives*, vol. I, Richmond, UK: Richmond, pp. 61–88.

Rist, Alexander and Eggler, M. (1992), 'Overview of Proposal for CO_2 Taxation in Switzerland', in OECD, *Climate Change, Designing a Practical Tax System*, Paris, pp. 55–63.

Rose-Ackerman, S. (1973), 'Effluent Charges: A Critique', *Canadian Journal of Economics*, 6 (4), 512–528.

Runge, Ford C. and Jones, Tom (1996), 'Subsidies, Tax Incentives and the Environment: An Overview and Synthesis', in OECD, *Subsidies and Environment: Exploring the Linkages*, Paris, pp. 7–21.

Schelling, Thomas C. (1983), 'Prices as Regulatory Instruments', in Thomas C. Schelling (ed.), *Incentives for Environmental Protection*, Cambridge, MA and London, UK: The MIT Press, pp. 1–40.

Schnutenhaus, Jörn O. (1995), 'Tax Differentials for Catalytic Converters and Unleaded Petrol in Germany', in Robert Gale and Stephan Barg with Alexander

Gillies (eds), *Green Budget Reform: An International Casebook of Leading Practices*, London: Earthscan Publications, pp. 79–90.

Segerson, Kathleen (1996), 'Issues in the Choice of Environmental Policy Instruments', in John B. Braden, Henrik Folmer and Thomas S. Ulen (eds), *Environmental Policy with Political and Economic Integration: The European Union and the United States*, Cheltenham, UK and Brookfield, US: Edward Elgar, pp. 149–174.

Shavell, Steven (1984), 'Liability for Harm Versus Regulation of Safety', *Journal of Legal Studies*, 13, 357–374.

Smith, Stephen (1992), 'Taxation and the Environment: A Survey', *Fiscal Studies*, 13 (4), 21–57.

Smith, Stephen (1995), *'Green' Taxes and Charges: Policy and Practice in Britain and Germany*, London: The Institute for Fiscal Studies.

Smith, Stephen (1997), 'Environmental Tax Design', in Tim O'Riordan (ed.), *Ecotaxation*, London: Earthscan Publications, 21–36.

Smith, Stephen and Vollebergh, Herman (1993), 'The European Carbon Excise Proposal: A Green Tax Takes Shape', *EC Tax Review*, 4, 207–221.

SOU 1989:35, *Reformerad mervärdeskatt m.m.* (Reform of the Value-added Tax etc., Sweden), Stockholm.

SOU 1989:21, *Sätt värde på miljön – miljöavgifter på svavel och klor. Delbetänkande av miljöavgiftsutredningen*, (Setting a Value on the Environment – Environmental Charges on Sulphur and Chlorine. Part of the Report of the Environmental Charges Committee), Stockholm.

SOU 1989:83, *Ekonomiska styrmedel i miljöpolitiken: Energi och trafik*, (Economic Instruments in Environmental Policy. Energy and Transport), Stockholm.

SOU 1990:59, *Sätt värde på miljön! Miljöavgifter och andra ekonomiska styrmedel. Betänkande av miljöavgiftsutredningen*, (Setting a Value on the Environment! Environmental Charges and Other Economic Instruments. The Report of the Environmental Charges Committee), Stockholm.

SOU 1991:90, *Konkurrensneutral energibeskattning. Betänkande av utredningen om översyn av reglerna om skattenedsättning för industrin och växthusnäringen m.m.* (Competitively Neutral Energy Taxation. The Report Concerning the Tax Relief Rules on Indutry and Commercial Horticulture, etc.), Stockholm.

SOU 1993:118, *Morot och piska för bättre miljö. Förslag om utvidgad användning av ekonomiska styrmedel mot kväveoksidutsläpp. Betänkande av utredningen av ekonomiska styrmedel vad avser kväveoksider m.m.* (Stick and Carrot for Better Environment. Proposal for Extended Use of Economic Instruments on Nitrogen Oxides' Emissions. The Report of the Committee Analysing the Use of Economic Instruments with Respect to Nitrogen Oxides, etc.), Stockholm.

SOU 1994:114, *Avfallsfri framtid Betänkande av Avfallsskatteutredningen*, (Future Without Waste. The Report of the Waste Tax Committee), Stockholm.

Spackman, Michael (1997), 'Hypothetication: A View from the Treasury', in Tim O'Riordan (ed.), *Ecotaxation*, London: Earthscan Publications, pp. 45–51.

Stavins, Robert N. and Whitehead, Bradley W. (1992), *The Greening of America's Taxes: Pollution Charges and Environmental Protection*, Center for Science & International Affairs, Harvard University.

Stewart, R.B. (1981), 'Regulation, Innovation, and Administrative Law: A Conceptual Framework', *California Law Review*, 69, 1256–1377.

Stevens, Candice (1993), 'Synthesis Report: Environmental Policies and Industrial Competitiveness', in OECD, *Environmental Policies and Industrial Competitiveness*, Paris, pp. 7–20.

Stiglitz, Joseph E. (1988), *Economics of the Public Sector*, 2nd ed., W.W. Norton & Company, New York, London.

Surrey, Stanley (1973), *Pathways to Tax Reform: The Concept of Tax Expenditures*, Cambridge, MA: Harvard University Press.

Surrey, Stanley S. and McDaniels, Paul (1985), *Tax Expenditures*, Cambridge, MA, USA and London, UK: Harvard University Press.

TemaNord 1994:561, *The Use of Economic Instruments in Nordic Environmental Policy*, Nordic Council of Ministers, Oslo.

TemaNord 1996:568, *The Use of Economic Instruments in Nordic Environmental Policy*, Nordic Council of Ministers, Copenhagen.

Terkla, David (1984), 'The Efficiency Value of Effluent Tax Revenues', *Journal of Environmental Economics and Management*, 11, 107–123.

Terra, Ben (1988), *Sales Taxation: The Case of Value Added Tax in the European Community*, Deventer, Kluwer Law and Taxation Publishers.

Theeuwes, Jules (1991), 'Regulation or taxation', in D.J. Krann and Veld in't (eds), *Environmental Protection: Public and Private Choice*, Dordrecht, Boston and London: Kluwer Academic, pp. 51–69.

Tietenberg, T.H. (1990), 'Economic Instruments for Environmental Protection', *Oxford Review of Economic Policy*, 61, 17–33 .

Tinbergen, J. (1952), *On the Theory of Economic Policy*, Amsterdam: North-Holland Publishing Company.

Victor, David G. (1992), 'Practical Aspects of Implementing Greenhouse Taxes: Issues for OECD Countries', in OECD Documents, *Climate Change: Designing a Practical Tax System*, Paris, pp. 241–272.

Vollebergh, Herman R.J. (1994), 'Environmental Taxes and Transaction Costs', *Tinbergen Institute Discussion Paper no. 94–96*, Erasmus University Rotterdam.

Vos, Hans B. (1994), 'Economic Incentives in Environmental Policy: An Overview and Comparison of Their Use in New and Old EU Member States', in TemaNord 1994:647, *Economic Instruments in Environmental Policy – in a Europe without Border Control*, Nordic Council of Ministers, Copenhagen, pp. 8–26.

von Weitzäcker, Ernst U. and Jesinghaus, Jochen (1992), *Ecological Tax Reform: A Policy Proposal for Sustainable Development*, London, UK and New Jersey, USA: Zed Books.

Wenders, J.T. (1975), 'Methods of Pollution Control and the Rate of Change in Pollution Abatement Technology', *Water Resources Research*, 11, 383–396.

White, L.J. (1976), 'Effluent Charges as a Faster Means of Achieving Pollution Abatement', *Public Policy*, 24 (1), 111–125.

Whitehouse, Edward (1996), 'Tax Expenditures and Environmental Policy', in OECD, *Subsidies and Environment. Exploring the Linkages*, Paris, pp. 67–79.

Wienert, H. (1997), *Regulation and Industrial Competitiveness: A Perspective for Regulatory Reform*, Paris.

Wilkinson, Margaret (1994), 'Paying for Public Spending: Is There a Role for Earmarked Taxes?', *Fiscal Studies*, 15 (4), 119–135.

Yohe, G. (1976), 'Polluters' Profits and Political Response: Direct Control Versus Taxes: Comment', *The American Economic Review*, 65, 981–982.

Zeckhauser, Richard (1981), 'Preferred Policies When There is a Concern for Probability of Adoption', *Journal of Environmental Economics and Management*, 8, 215–237.

Index